Where in the World is My Team?

JOSSEY-BASS
A Wiley Imprint
www.josseybass.com

Where in the World is My Team?

MAKING A SUCCESS OF YOUR VIRTUAL

GLOBAL WORKPLACE

Terence Brake

A John Wiley and Sons, Ltd., Publication

Published in 2008 by   John Wiley & Sons Ltd, The Atrium, Southern Gate, Chichester, West Sussex PO19 8SQ, England

Telephone (+44) 1243 779777

Email (for orders and customer service enquiries): cs-books@wiley.co.uk
Visit our Home Page on www.wiley.com

Under the Jossey-Bass imprint, Jossey-Bass, 989 Market Street, San Francisco CA 94103-1741, USA
www.jossey-bass.com

Copyright © 2008 TMA World, 211 Piccadilly, London WIJ 9HF.
Telephone (+44) 2079 172784

Other Wiley Editorial Offices

John Wiley & Sons Inc., 111 River Street, Hoboken, NJ 07030, USA

Jossey-Bass, 989 Market Street, San Francisco, CA 94103-1741, USA

Wiley-VCH Verlag GmbH, Boschstr. 12, D-69469 Weinheim, Germany

John Wiley & Sons Australia Ltd, 42 McDougall Street, Milton, Queensland 4064, Australia

John Wiley & Sons (Asia) Pte Ltd, 2 Clementi Loop #02-01, Jin Xing Distripark, Singapore 129809

John Wiley & Sons Canada Ltd, 6045 Freemont Blvd, Mississauga, ONT, L5R 4J3, Canada

Wiley also publishes its books in a variety of electronic formats. Some content that appears in print may not be available in electronic books.

Library of Congress Cataloging-in-Publication Data

A catalogue record for this book in available from the Library of Congress

British Library Cataloguing in Publication Data

A catalogue record for this book is available from the British Library

ISBN 978-0-470-71429-4

Typeset in 11 on 13 pt ITC Garamond Light by SNP Best-set Typesetter Ltd., Hong Kong

Printed and bound in Great Britain by TJ International Ltd, Padstow, Cornwall, UK

This book is printed on acid-free paper responsibly manufactured from sustainable forestry in which at least two trees are planted for each one used for paper production.

To my global virtual family and those technologies that help keep us close

CONTENTS

ACKNOWLEDGEMENTS

After ten years of working virtually, I thought it was time to write a book.

BUT …

I didn't want to *read* another business book, let alone *write* one. If it was going to happen, I would have to find a way to write something useful *and* have fun. A number of TMA World people came on the journey, and I owe them my deepest thanks.

Chris Crosby, Managing Director, who was up for the idea of something different. He stayed the course when he wasn't sure where it was going.

Hans van der Linden, Global Account Director, whom I can't thank enough for his undying virtual enthusiasm. You kept me going Hans when I doubted I could pull it off.

Claire Lyell, Director of Strategic Partnerships, who became a great fan of the book, even though she felt the eroticism was rather tame.

Steven Parkinson, Sales and Marketing Director, who came in late to the project, but could immediately see the possibilities.

Laurie Quinn, Art Director, who I've known as a friend and colleague for more years than I care to think about. Thanks once again for your commitment to working tirelessly when the pressure is on. When is it off, you might be asking!

I'd also like to thank other colleagues in TMA World for their ongoing support:

Steve Pritchard and Russell Harlow, two world-class facilitators who not only educate others to be successful in global teams, but who walk the talk. Also, the two keystones in the TMA arch, Sandra May and Lyndsey Wills. I must also give a big thanks to the scores of TMA World associates around the world who do us proud every day.

Grateful thanks also to my good friend Akshina Samtani, who joined me as an intern from Georgetown University. She researched exhaustively, read the first drafts, contributed valuable insights, and would tell me 'It's perfect!' when I needed to hear that. Akshina also introduced me to Chicken Makani. She has become a much-loved member of our global extended family.

I first met Simone Alder when she was a student in one of my classes at the Summer Institute for Intercultural Communication (SIIC) in Portland, Oregon. While finishing her MA thesis on nonverbal communication in a global virtual team, she applied her clear, analytical mind to the book. Although she kept apologising for her 'direct German feedback', she contributed exactly what was needed and at the right time.

Many thanks also to my good friends Ros and Paul Taylor in Scotland who shared wonderful stories about their grandchildren. Tell me more!

Thanks also to TMA World's global clients who contribute so much by allowing me to play in their worlds. Many thanks also to the thousands of participants in TMA World's workshops, who learn from us and teach us in return.

These acknowledgements wouldn't be complete without a deep thanks to TMA World's business partners, Cartus, Future Work Institute (FWI), Global English, and others. You not only bring new opportunities but you also add new dimensions to my thinking. A special thanks to Margaret Regan and her wonderful associates at the Future Work Institute (FWI). The way you are launching yourselves and your vision into Second Life is inspiring. You are building the future one innovative, virtual brick at a time.

Dianne, my beautiful wife of 30 years, actually read this book and liked it! The fact that she was sitting by a pool on the gorgeous island of St Lucia at the time might have helped. Thanks D for your unfailing love and support. Never forgetting, of course, Morgan, Kristin, Wyatt, Ella, and Wren; Sam and Nicole; and Ben and Julie. You know who you are and how much I love you – face-to-face and virtually.

CAST OF CHARACTERS

INSIDE *THE FUN HOUSE*

Alain Badeau — Project Manager (Paris)

Corbishley Binks — So-called Director of Communications (London)

Maarten Bleeker — Somebody having something to do with budgets (Amsterdam)

Sadie Bryant — Public Relations Specialist (London) and Will's ex-girlfriend

Robert Chang — Regional Director, Americas (San Francisco) and Instant Messenger from unusual places

Mitchell Crabtree — Budget Director (London); also known as Gloom & Doom or just G&D

Geoff Dyson — Head of Game Innovation (London); also known as the Diceman

Alice Evans — Special Effects Designer (London) and potential love interest for Will

Daavid Gustafsson	User Interface Designer (Helsinki)
Sheila Hetherington-Etheridge	Managing Director (London); also known as SHE
Moonbeam Jones	Office Manager and 'mystic' (London)
Art Kelly	Founder of *The Fun House* company
Aki Kwon	Head of Market Development, Asia (Hong Kong)
Sunil Mehta	Regional Director, Asia (Bangalore, India) and *Fun House* intellectual
Webster Rushkoff	Game Tester (London); also known as The Bugster
Nisha Shenoy	Manager of Human Resources (London) and maker of the mega-divine Chicken Makani
Shakespeare Spinks	Budget Supervisor for Projects and the bane of Will's existence
Emily Wagner	Project Manager (New York)
Anton Weiss	Project Manager (Berlin)
Will Williams	Personal Assistant to SHE and our guide to the global workplace
Ruth Wilson	Global Marketing Director (London) and exhausted mother of the dreaded Davian

OUTSIDE *THE FUN HOUSE*

Bess Avebury — Will's New Age therapist sister; married to Noel and mother of Emily and Sebastian, the Purgatory Twins

Truman Beardsley — American global management consultant and friend of Sunil's

Daniel Collins — Will's ex-best friend; married to Sadie

Paula Fowler — Business journalist and sociopath

Tomas and Theresa Lustig — Principals in Boffin Labs; designers of the Global Office Workspace known in *The Fun House* as Go*dz*W*illa*

Sophie James — New and serious love in Will's life discovered via the Internet

Beverly Williams — Will's mother and *grande dame* of the amateur stage

Gareth Williams — Will's father, retired history teacher and passionate devotee of Roman ruins

WELCOME MAT

Introducing Will Williams, our guide through the global workplace.

LONDON

Call me Will. The full name is William Williams, but the last thing I'm into is formality. I recently joined *The Fun House* as assistant to our fearless leader, so I'm still what they call a *newbie*.

Before *The Fun House*, I'd left the UK to study for an MBA in New York. I survived by scraping just enough money together in bartending to pay for rent, food, and one trip to a film (*sans* popcorn) every other week. When I returned to London, I found the MBA was helpful in getting me through *The Fun Palace* portal – that's what we call the front door to our office – but once inside I was confronted with the messy non-MBA Real World or, in *Fun Palace* terminology, the RW.

What do we do in the RW? We design games for the Virtual World or VW. What is considered RW and VW gets a little fuzzy around here as you might imagine. Inside *The Fun House* they don't call us employees, but *players*.

We develop games by working virtually with colleagues and partners worldwide. The Technical Lead might be in the UK, Art Director in Japan, Special Effects and User Interface Leads on the West Coast of the USA, Lead Environment Artist on the East Coast, Game Director in Finland, … and so on. It's what I've learned here at *The Fun House* about working virtually that I want to share with you, and to do that I'm letting you peek inside entries I made in my e-journal during a recent project. I've organized them into a framework suggested by one of my colleagues in India (The Six Cs of Global Team Collaboration). Yes, he was a management consultant in a previous life!

You might think because I'm working in a computer game company and that I'm going to tell you about working virtually, that I'm some kind of geek-freak (or *geef* as I call them). Well, that wouldn't be true. What I'm trying to say is that you won't have to crawl through a parched desert of technical jargonese on my account. I have a smart phone, an iPod, a digital camera, a laptop, and a wireless setup in my pathetic excuse for a flat in north London, but, I'm no *geef*. I also play around on *Myspace, Facebook, Flickr, Second Life, Wikipedia, YouTube, del.icio.us, Digg, StumbleUpon,* and *PostSecret.com*, as well as other sites that help me stay up-to-date, publish, broadcast, connect, personalize, expose myself, and – let's face it – have fun. None of those make me a *geef*, just your average Web 2.0er.

Do you need to know any more about me at this point? Well, if you ask my sister Bess, the New Age therapist, she'll say that I'm a young soul and adrift from my inner guide. She'll also say I lack self-awareness, that I avoid conflict, and have a neurotic need to be loved. Apparently, I also tend to use humour as a defence mechanism. Last time she came to visit me I said, 'So, where did you park your *karma?*' which I thought was hilarious. She just gave me that despairing elder sister look meaning, 'Oh Will, grow up.'

Anyway, what I'm going to share with you started a few weeks ago on a bitter-bleak autumn morning in London. Having spent 30 minutes rocking violently in an overcrowded Underground train with my face trapped between the steaming armpits of those standing on either side of me, I was well primed for learning more about what I came to know as the new workplace.

LET THE GAMES BEGIN

THE PROJECT

'WILL!'

SHE called me into her office this am before I'd even had a chance to log on to our Global Office Workspace environment, affectionately known to us all as GO*dz*W*illa*, and even before I'd been able to sit and savour my full-fat, high-octane latte, fondly known to me as the Caffeine Tornado or CT. Excellent brew! If I could buy shares in *Has Bean* – the corner coffee shop where I hand over an exorbitant amount of cash for it each morning – I most definitely would.

'Morning, SHE.'

'Hi Will, take a seat.' She looked longingly at my CT until I relented and gave it to her. *Note to self: look for a good assertiveness training programme.*

Now before I go on, I don't want you thinking I'm insulting my boss by calling her SHE. Almost everyone calls her SHE. Those are her initials – Sheila Hetherington-Etheridge. She was brought into *The Fun House* two years ago by the original founder to take over as Managing Director. He's now living on an island somewhere off the coast of Africa. When SHE arrived the organization needed more professional management if it was to continue its three-digit growth while becoming more profitable. SHE has made a huge impact, and there's absolutely no shortage of respect for her.

'I have an interesting assignment for you Will,' she said, and I was instantly on my guard. *Interesting assignment*, I had learned quickly, was SHE code for next to impossible assignment, and, as a consequence, my personal life was about to slide into a horrendous decline. Ha! I apologize – that last statement is wildly misleading because my personal life is next to NONEXISTENT!

'I had a call from a TV station on Friday night,' SHE said, 'and they want me to do an interview in about six weeks on the new workplace.' There was an uncomfortable silence while I waited for more information. None came.

'Ah yes, the new workplace,' I said as confidently as I could, not wanting to lose face.

'Yes … come on Will. You know, working together globally via technology.' Obviously my confident response hadn't been confident enough and I'd let her see my puzzlement. *Note to self: also look for a training programme on bluffing more effectively.*

'Groupware, videoconferencing, web meetings,' she continued. 'All the cool stuff we can no longer live without. What I want is for you to put together a briefing report for me. You haven't been here very long and I think this will be a great opportunity for you to get to know the business better.' More SHE code – *great opportunity* is close cousin to *interesting assignment!*

'Schedule a few virtual *Indaba*[1] sessions when you can with …'

'Sorry, what? Did you say *in … da … ba?*' I stuttered.

'I did. It's one of those words that Art Kelly (the founder) brought back from Africa on his last trip. I think it's a Zulu word meaning *forum*. Basically it's a tribal meeting to discuss an important question, although I think the way Art uses it is to mean "seeking knowledge together". In the meantime, you should probably talk with Sunil Mehta in Bangalore; he's our in-house intellectual *extraordinaire*.'

---

[1] *Indaba* is a real Zulu word. I didn't make it up. I looked it up on Answers. com. It originated in South Africa where Zulu chiefs would call their people together for meetings on important issues. Nelson Mandela's African National Congress used the word for its meetings.

'But wait,' I protested. 'If you've been asked to talk about this on TV, don't you know it already?'

'Just because we work in the new way doesn't mean we've thought about it very much. I need you to articulate what we do. Ciao Will. Call you when I need you.'

SHE always said *ciao* when she had finished with me, which I found really annoying. She said it kept her in touch with her inner Italian. Her great-great-great grandfather was Italian!

Leaving SHE's office, my head felt like it was full of grazing sheep. I was definitely missing the lightning jolt from the CT. There was no time to go and get another one so I raided the bag of chocolate-covered espresso beans I knew were in Shakespeare Spinks' desk drawer, my office neighbour. Well, it was an emergency!

He's an odd duck is Spinks. He works on finances with Mitchell Crabtree. Spinks has slipped well into middle age before his thirties, and he carries the air of the landed gentry about him. Much of the time he dresses his round freckled frame in fashions suitable for the Duke of Edinburgh on a duck hunt (an olde worlde fashion tsunami I've heard SHE call him). I prefer *Young Farmer Chic*. Tweeds, corduroy, check shirts, knitted ties, and woolly jumpers – that sort of thing.

I hear from others that he was actually born and raised in an industrial town up North (not in the countryside as he pretends) and that he had ambitious working class parents who scrimped and saved to send him to third-rate private schools where he excelled in superiority and back-stabbing. When he's not trying to put you down to others, he goes on about our glorious island's heritage, or he drivels on the phone about something called the Anglo-Saxon Alliance (must be a fantasy game he's working the budgets for).

What someone like Spinks is doing in the wacky world of *The Fun House*, I really don't know. He's well past his expiration date. By the way, what parents call their son,

Shakespeare Spinks? Come to think of it, what parents call their son William Williams? *Note to self: ask my therapist sister if parents who give their children such alliterative names have a recognized mental condition?*

Before leaving and braving those armpits in my face again – which at this point in the day have had plenty of time to ripen – I e-mailed Sunil in Bangalore telling him about the new workplace project and asking for a good date and time to talk.

STARTING OUT

I kept my CT hidden in a paper bag this morning. Spinks asked me if I had seen anyone going into his desk drawers – his supply of chocolate espresso beans was 'frightfully diminished, don't you know'. 'No,' I answered without a hint of shame. *Note to self: might not need training programme on bluffing after all.* He muttered something about not being able to trust anyone in this country anymore, and then he wandered off to find someone from Maintenance who could replace the desk key he had lost last week. Actually, his lost key was in my desk drawer. I feel it is my solemn duty to torture Spinks – in a therapeutic way, of course. He takes himself far too seriously, and his know-it-all-ism makes me squirm. Think of a hypodermic needle about to puncture one of your eyeballs and you'll know how I feel about Spinks.

Received e-mail from Sunil that I can talk to him tomorrow morning. Things are moving.

Spinks returned with a new key and perched himself on the end of my desk. 'I'm sure you and I will be great friends Will,' he said in his pompous way. 'I hear Sheila has given you an assignment on the evolving workplace. Jolly good. I'm well versed in the techno, thingy stuff, so please know that you can turn to me for help at any time. The likes of us chaps,' he said, trying to wink a bulbous eye, 'have to stick together, if you know what I mean.'

I didn't, but decided not to pursue it. I knew that asking Spinks for input was tantamount to handing him the project and him taking the credit. No way!

'You could also talk with my friend Paula Fowler,' he went on. 'She's an up-and-coming business journalist who's becoming terrifically well respected by all in the know. We grew up in the country together. Pretty filly as well.' A respected journalist who is a 'pretty filly', I mused. Political correctness – or anything remotely like it – obviously isn't on the Shakespeare Spinks radar screen.

It isn't just Spinks' phony upper-class style that pulls my chain. I also have a deep distrust of him – a weasel is what we call his breed in Britain. I had learned soon after joining *The Fun House* that Spinks had amorous longings for SHE and that he'd really wanted my job so that he could work more closely with her. Apparently he'd been making snide suggestions to her that my capabilities might not be up to completing the new workplace project, that *he* would be much more adept. I'd found this out from Moonbeam Jones, our pink-haired, body-pierced, anti-glam, and tattooed Office Manager (obviously with a name like Moonbeam, a child of aged hippies).

I couldn't imagine a friend of Spinks as someone I would want involved with the project, but I also felt it couldn't hurt to get an intelligent outside perspective (the word 'pretty' didn't hurt either). I dropped Paula Fowler an e-mail seeing if she could meet me for a chat. Got an almost spontaneous reply: *Sorry, drinks impossible. It will have to be breakfast the day after tomorrow. Meet me at Le Petit-Déjeuner, 07:30. Wear red carnation so I can spot you easily and not waste time having to guess who you are.* Straightforward, I thought. I was a bit puzzled by the mention of 'drinks', not having put forward that suggestion.

I also sent Maarten Bleecker in Amsterdam an e-mail saying that I would call him at half eight my time the next day. I needed some information about the euro budget.

I SHOULD HAVE STAYED UNDER THE BLANKETS

Got in at 8:15 this morning ready to talk with Maarten. There was already a message from him on my VoIP[2] system in GO*dz*W*illa* asking where I was? Damn cheek, I thought, having got up especially early and missing breakfast. I called him back.

'Hello Maarten. Its 8:15 here, I'm early,' I said coolly.

'Hello Will. It's 9:15 here. What's your point?'

'I said I would call you at half eight my time.'

'That's correct.'

'So, it's not half past eight yet!'

'Half eight is 7:30 here – a half of eight! I got up early and missed breakfast,' he responded with a definite edge to his voice.

'I'm sorry Maarten, I didn't realize,' I said apologetically. 'I missed my breakfast as well if it's any consolation.'

'It isn't. Just tell me what you need.'

After treading on eggshells for the rest of my call with Maarten, I checked my e-mails.

There was one from Paula: *Forget the carnation. You might have trouble finding one this time of year. Just tell me what you look like.*

I complied, although my tongue was most definitely in my cheek as I did so: *Engagingly handsome. Above average height, and just a little over average weight. Light brown hair that tends to flop over my right eye in seductive strands. Good posture, good teeth, and a smile that will melt your heart. A Jude Law with a bit more muscle.*

It's my theory that women like men who make them laugh. I don't know why I hang on to that belief after the relationship *Titanics* I've sunk.

Paula e-mailed back quickly: *I hope you're more intelligent in person. Just wear a carnation!*

---

[2]VoIP – Voice over Internet Protocol. A technology that enables calls to be made through a broadband Internet connection.

FACE TO FACE AIN'T ALL IT'S CRACKED UP TO BE

I'd managed to find a red carnation in a *very* expensive flower shop. Hopefully, I could claim it as an expense. Not wanting to attract strange looks on the Underground, I'd kept the carnation in my coat pocket, and it didn't travel well! Arriving at *Le Petit-Déjeuner* five minutes late, I realized I didn't have a buttonhole in my leather jacket and so had to carry the poor crushed thing inside. The interior of the restaurant was dark and so I had to walk around all of the tables hoping that Paula would recognize the stalk in my hand as a red carnation. Talk about embarrassing!

'I suppose you're William,' a sharp voice said from a corner table. 'You're late. I despise people who waste my time. Sit down.' I did as I was told while offering apologies. 'Don't snivel,' she said. 'I'm assuming you've read my articles on the new world of work.'

'Actually, no,' I confessed. She contorted her face into such a grimace that only the whites of her eyes showed between her heavily lined eyelids. This was not only terrifying to me, but also to the waitress who dropped her pen and notepad into Paula's decaffeinated Cappuccino. Paula squealed like a cat whose tail was caught in a hot toaster and cursed the waitress in language that would make a rapper blush. The poor love ran off in tears looking for the manager. It took me some time to apologize for Paula, who obviously didn't have 'I apologize' in her vocabulary. The manager asked for no more disturbances and kindly let us stay as long as Paula would control herself.

I looked at Paula closely. Spinks had used 'pretty' and 'smart' to describe her. 'Pretty' I could see in a *Goth Chic* kind of way: long black hair framing a high cheek-boned and untouched-by-the-evil-sun face, and deep sea-blue eyes. She had thick mascara covering her eyelashes, dark green eye shadow, and deep red – almost black – lips that were a bit thin for my taste. While she was small, she was wonderfully well proportioned, if you know what I mean. And the figure-hugging, cleavage-popping black dress … well, it was almost too much for this lonely, tormented soul to bear.

'Smart' was more of a challenge. Smart in terms of grey matter maybe, but people smart and judgement – hmm – jury likely to return life-without-parole on that one. 'I suppose you must have lots of these power breakfasts,' I said, trying to pick up the conversation after the whites-of-the-eyes debacle.

'To be a *power* breakfast,' she shot back, '*all* of the participants would need to possess *some* modicum of power. I do, you don't, so your statement is meaningless.' I decided to let Paula control the conversation in her own way.

Nibbling at her fruit plate and plain yogurt, Paula got down to business. 'As you haven't read my articles, I suppose I'll have to give you the whole lecture,' she said resentfully. 'Soooo tedious!'

'To begin with,' she hissed, 'there are two major forces shaping today's workplace. The first is globalization and the second is new communications and computing technology. The first has made commercial and labour borders largely irrelevant and the second has enabled us to create a global workplace.' She sounded like an audio version of a business textbook – clear and concise, but as appealing as a used tea bag.

I started to say 'And what about ...?' but she hammered me shut with 'Don't interrupt me until I'm done!' *Note to self: should ask Paula to recommend assertiveness training programme.*

'Now, these two forces of globalization and technology change everything. Think about the complexity of today's world for a business manager working across multiple geographies with different market needs and tastes, different regulatory systems, varied environmental conditions, disruptive technological change, and, of course, deeply embedded cultural values, beliefs, and behaviours that may clash with our own.'

'Very interesting,' I said, to which her reply was 'I told you not to interrupt me. You're not much of a listener are you?' On and on she went like Tantric sex: 'Given this complexity, we find that paradox, uncertainty, and ambiguity are the norm for managers. It's a wonder we're able to do any business at all. Now speak.'

'Oh … oh, thank you,' I stuttered. 'So … Paula, how should we manage this … this complexity?'

'We do what human beings have done throughout history when we haven't been trying to kill one another – we collaborate.' It was very hard for me to imagine Paula collaborating with anyone. She seemed perfect for starting wars, but collaboration?

'Each person,' she went on, 'brings insights, knowledge, and skills into the workspace and we navigate our way through the complexity together. As we do, we generate knowledge and channel it into new products and services. It's knowledge transformed into innovation that drives business success today.'

'So what you mean is … ,' I tried to say. Again she cut me off. 'First,' she said, 'I didn't ask you to speak and, second, my meaning is perfectly clear and is unlikely to benefit from your interpretative skills. Now let me continue … competitive edge in today's world resides in what we have in our brains and how we exchange, rework, distribute, and absorb what is there. The real competitive power is when our ideas, knowledge, and expertise intersect with others and create new possibilities that we had not imagined individually. Competitive advantage is now coupled with collaborative advantage.'

She hardly paused to take a breath. I thought I might lose the will to live. 'The key question is what can we do to ensure we collaborate successfully across space and time? Technology is just the medium, the tool. We must make our collaborative technologies effective, but we must go deeper if we want to work together successfully. We talk a lot about connectivity in today's digital world, but it is human connectivity that counts – our ability to understand and respect one another, our ability to negotiate ways of working together.'

I think my mouth was hanging open too long on hearing Paula say words like *understand* and *respect* because she got up from her chair and said, 'I'm leaving if you're going to be sick.' She fled the restaurant as though escaping the plague, leaving me to pay the bill. She is the most powerful case made yet for working at a distance, I thought to myself. Dragging my traumatized self back to the Underground I thought of the wondrous diversity of human beings, and how, sometimes, I wish it was less so.

SUNIL'S *MANDALA*

I reached Sunil via VoIP on GO*dz*W*illa*. 'Hello Sunil, thanks for your time.'

'My pleasure, William.'

'SHE is going to be interviewed on TV, and she would like your help in talking about the new workplace.'

'I'll do what I can,' Sunil said modestly. 'Let me see if I can put a frame around this for you. I like to talk about my Team Mandala, which is a model I developed while I was working as a management consultant in the US.'

'Team Mandala?' I asked.

'Yes, sorry William. Let me explain. *Mandala* is a Sanskrit word meaning "circle" although I have taken the liberty of designing mine as a hexagon. Each Mandala teaches different lessons. You might have seen a film of Buddhist monks creating them out of coloured sand. When they're finished they just get swept away.'

'No … haven't seen that one,' I said. 'Who's in it?' If truth be told, I wasn't too happy at this point. It sounded way too New Age for me – something I had more than enough of from my sister Bess. 'It sounds very interesting Sunil, but I don't think this is quite the input I'm looking for,' I said politely.

'Don't be too hasty in your judgements William,' said Sunil. 'I'm going to e-mail you something right now.'

His e-mail attachment was a diagram called The Six Cs of Global Team Collaboration. 'That looks like something I can relate to,' I said more enthusiastically.

'I thought you might find this more palatable, William,' Sunil laughed, and walked me through the model. 'This is my Team Mandala in Western clothes. You can see six performance zones for global team success: Cooperation, Convergence, Coordination, Capability, Communication, and Cultural Intelligence. In today's world Collaboration has six Cs in it. Underneath the diagram you'll find a short description of each Performance Zone.'

'Thanks Sunil. Can you hold on while I read through them?'

'Certainly, William.'

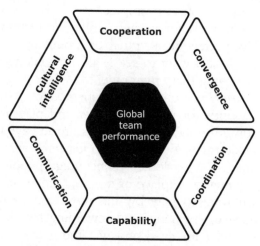

The Six Cs of Global Collaboration.

1. **Cooperation:** ability to develop and maintain trusting relationships across geographies, time zones, and cultures.
2. **Convergence:** ability to maintain a clear purpose, direction, and shared set of priorities.

3. **Coordination:** ability to align work through clearly defined roles and responsibilities, shared tools, processes, and methods.
4. **Capability:** ability to leverage the knowledge, skills, and experiences of *all* members, and increase the capabilities of the team as a whole.
5. **Communication:** ability to generate shared verbal and written understandings across distances via technology.
6. **Cultural Intelligence:** ability to develop and maintain a global virtual workplace inclusive of value and style differences.

'I like this very much,' I said, 'OK if I use it?'

'Most certainly.'

Before we finished the call, I asked Sunil if he had any other thoughts to share about the new workplace?

'Virtual architecture,'[3] he said after a pause.

'Er … yes. Go on,' I prompted.

'Every time we interact with others via technology, we are collectively creating a virtual environment around and between us. What I want to see is all of us taking responsibility for designing that environment.

'In our *Fun House* business, we spend a lot of time creating virtual worlds for people to enter and play around in. As you know, the players themselves are involved increasingly in transforming our game worlds into ones that suit their own needs. Why don't we encourage people to think about their virtual workplace as a virtual game-space? What rules do we want to play by and how can we make the game immersive, engaging, and rewarding for all of us so that we stay fully involved and win the game – or in the case of business, achieve our objectives?'

'That's an awesome idea,' I said, immediately feeling embarrassed for having said awesome out loud – a linguistic

---

[3] Virtual architecture is used here in relation to 'designing' any virtual space between technologically linked workers, and not just in relation to those found in virtual worlds like Second Life.

leftover from my time in the States. 'So, on a global project team, one of their first tasks would be to design the virtual workplace in which they are going to work?'

'Absolutely, why not?' he said. 'I'm not saying every team needs to create a unique virtual world for themselves, just that they need to pay closer attention to their virtual space. Sorry William,' he continued, 'I'm already late for another call. Good luck with the project. Call me again if you think I can be helpful.'

'Many thanks Sunil. Wonderful to talk with you.'

GO*dz*Willa

It's not exactly the virtual work game-space that Sunil has in mind, but GO*dz*W*illa* is a step in that direction. It's our Global Office Workspace, the world where everyone in *The Fun House* works each day, no matter where they're located in the RW. It's a shared virtual space where we work individually and together. There is even a café called *The Wit's End Café* where we – the frazzled multitaskers and blitzed continuous partial attention[4] cyborgs – can meet for a casual drink and a chat.

If we have such a virtual workspace, why aren't we all working from the RW places we call 'home'? *The Fun House* did start as a virtual organization, but it soon became clear that some people needed a physical location – bricks, mortar, and actual windows (not just Microsoft's). I'm glad I'm not imprisoned in my one room flat with the pull-down-from-the-wall-bed and charity shop desk and chair. I work at

---

[4] A term coined by Linda Stone (co-founder of Microsoft's Virtual World's Group, now the Social Computing Group). It is a state of continuous stimulation in which we might be attending to one task, but always tuned into background information and/or opportunities that could be more interesting or urgent – attention, therefore, is always partial. We are always on high alert. It is a result of being in an always-on world in which feeling alive is to feel connected and where we are driven not to miss anything that could be important to us.

home sometimes, but it's good to be in the RW with all its sights, smells, tastes, noises, and working toilets.

YOU COULD HAVE KNOCKED ME DOWN WITH A VIRTUAL FEATHER!

Just a few days after my meeting with Paula, she e-mailed me. I was beyond speechless: *Hi Will. Thank you for breakfast. How is the project going?*

I couldn't think of anything to say beyond: *Hi. Thanks for asking. It's going well.*

Perhaps in my desire to win people over and be liked by everyone, I attached The Six Cs of Global Team Collaboration with a brief explanation. Do I really have an unconscious desire to be liked by everyone, even Paula? No, I'm not that much of a masochist? Am I?

And who *is* this Paula person? Personal identity – what is that? Is the face-to-face Paula a totally different being from the softer and fluffier digital Paula? Can you point at anyone and say with certainty this is who *you* are? Or even, this is who *I* am. Steady on lad, getting in too deep.

LUNCH WITH SADIE

I had lunch with Sadie Bryant, my ex-girlfriend from university. Sadie has been working in *The Fun House* for about two years and is our Public Relations Specialist. Actually, she helped me get the personal assistant job when I returned from New York.

I met her during my second year at university. Intelligent, independent, daring, and mind-numbingly Tyra Banks beautiful, she was everything I ever wanted. I really wasn't mature enough to commit at the time (maybe I'm still not) so she eventually broke up with me. While I was in New York she married my best friend Daniel Collins. I hate him with every molecule of my being!

Sadie and I met in a small café near the office called *No Regrets*. Ha! 'Tell me about what you're doing for SHE,' she said. 'Working virtually leaves me SCREAMING at the walls most of the time,' she spat while losing control of her fork and launching a cherry tomato in my direction.

'I can see you have feelings about this topic, Sadie my love. What's the problem?' While I waited for her response, I tried oh so carefully to remove the oil and vinegar drenched tomato out of my lap, but the pesky thing kept slipping out of my grasp and smearing the front of my best khaki trousers. I knew I was in for an afternoon of embarrassing stares and pathetic jokes.

'You can put in place all the technology you want,' Sadie went on, oblivious to my lap dancing tomato war, 'but you're still working with real people with all their quirky likes and dislikes, petty jealousies, power plays, neuroses, and paranoia, and, in the meantime, you're trying to get your work done across multiple time zones and cultures. It's a bloody nightmare!'

'Have you ever had a good experience?' I asked.

She played with the remaining cherry tomatoes on top of her Romaine salad while I prepared myself for the next oily assault. 'I suppose the *Warmonger* team worked pretty well.'

'And what made that different?' I asked, as she reached for her mobile phone that was melodically chiming the opening bars of a *Lily Allen* song. She gestured for me to wait while she answered a call from Daniel. How much I hate him; let me count the ways!

'Daniel says "Hi",' she said after finishing the call. I smiled weakly. 'You wanted to know what made the *Warmonger* team different. I think it was the leadership of Robert Chang in San Francisco. He really helped us come together.'

'Robert is Regional Director for the Americas, right?'

'Yes.'

'How did he help you work together?' I asked, while attacking my Gorgonzola cheese and onion salad with gusto. A truly potent mix of tastes!

'I think Robert was very good at recognizing that every virtual team faces at least three main challenges,' she said while trying to spear her last tomato, 'and that you really need to pay attention to them all of the time.'

'Go on.'

'Isolation first,' she said. 'When there is reduced communication people start getting anxious or alienated and mentally switch off or become resentful. I've learned the hard way that paranoia and hostility love to breed in silent spaces. There's also the fact you're not so able to "read" people virtually. Usually there are very few clues about what someone is really thinking or feeling.'

'What else?'

'Well, related to isolation is fragmentation. It's hard to maintain a sense of team cohesion. There are often gaps and overlaps, and, of course, there are the challenges of different approaches and styles.'

'And the third?'

'Confusion. I think working at a distance can make fools of us all. Misunderstandings caused by lack of shared backgound or vague communication, conflicting assumptions, and lack of transparency. I recently had an e-mail from someone in the States who said he had created a "strawman" agenda for our upcoming meeting and that he had a "hard-stop" at 3 pm his time. I had no clue what he meant and I spent at least twenty minutes trying to find out. He could have just said that he had put together a preliminary agenda and that he must finish by 3 pm.'

'But aren't these problems that can happen on a face-to-face team as well?' I asked.

'Yes, of course. It's just that when you work virtually, a problem can easily be blown out of proportion. So Robert liked all of us to ask, "Is what I'm doing and how I'm doing it supporting Engagement, Cohesion, and Clarity?" But enough about work; tell me what's going on in your life, Will.'

'It's OK,' I said, which was a lie. I was pretty much in despair about all things in general. No sex life, football team struggling to win away from home, few friends left in London, rain, damp, and what amounted to a mouldy cupboard for a place to live.

'Only OK! Poor Will. What's missing?' she asked.

I couldn't help myself. 'You,' I replied mournfully.

'Oh shut up,' she said, smiling. 'Stuff that industrial waste you call a salad in your face and let's get back to work.'

When I left the office that night, Spinks was on the phone talking about the Anglo-Saxon Alliance. I thought I knew all of the fantasy games under development. I'll have to ask around to find out more.

OH NO, NO, NO, NO, NO!

Waiting for me in the office this morning was another e-mail from Paula: *Hi Will. Thanks for sending The Six Cs. Perhaps we can get together for a drink to talk more about them.*

What, what, what? Drinks with Paula! Noooooooo, I don't think so! I e-mailed her back: *Hi Paula, Drinks? I'm afraid I'm allergic to any form of alcohol. Makes me break out in horrific pustules. Sorry.*

There was an immediate reply: *Will, You poor thing. I have a wonderful allergist. I'm going to give her a ring and have her contact you.*

Oh no. Save me.

I bumped into SHE as I was leaving. 'Hi Will, how's it going?' she said in her voice that I can only describe as champagne – optimistic, energetic, forever young.

Spinks passed us on his way out. His little snake eyes slimed all over her and I could feel the jealousy oozing out of him as he slithered past me to the lift.

COOPERATION

LAST CHANCE FOR LOVE?

I can't believe I did it, but after my lunch with Sadie, I decided to search for a soul mate (or any mate) on the Internet. Call me a loser, I don't care. Went to LoveNest.com and completed a personal profile. It's exciting in a weird way. Like everyone else – surely – I've played around in social networking sites like *MySpace, LinkedIn, Friendster, Bebo,* and *Facebook,* but … nothing! My space is an empty space, or so it seems.

THIS THING CALLED TRUST

I bumped into Mitchell Crabtree in *Has Bean* at lunchtime while I was picking up my second Caffeine Tornado of the morning (had been up for a 4 am teleconference). Crabtree is *The Fun House* Budget Director and probably the oldest person in the organization. He must be at least 50. Tall, thin, stooped, and with longish graying hair, he reminds me of a Dickens character. Most of *The Fun House* players refer to him as G&D (Gloom & Doom).

'Good to see you Will. How are you settling in?' he asked during a spasm of raucous coughing. I could tell by the smell of his clothes and his yellowed fingers that he was a heavy smoker.

'Great. I enjoy what I'm doing, and the people are a cool bunch to work with.'

'Glad to hear it, but don't walk around with your eyes closed.' He stopped to take a breath and clear his throat. It sounded less like a clearing and more like stampeding toads in runny custard.

'Eyes closed? Not sure I understand,' I said.

'Stay alert. You're young and you have this aura of innocence about you,' he said, 'but people are people whether they appear *cool* or not. They've all got their own self-interests and agendas. People are people the world over – envy, greed, vanity, pride. You can't change them. Shouldn't bother trying.'

'I see. Anyone in particular I should look out for?' Shakespeare Spinks immediately came to mind.

'All of 'em. Take my advice, trust no one, and murder before suicide. Those are lessons I learned early on.'

'That sounds radical. Don't people have their good sides as well?' I asked.

There was another toad stampede in his chest before he went on. 'You've got a lot to learn my friend. They'll spear you with a smile as soon as look at you. Look after yourself, no one else.' He handed over money to the cashier for his small black coffee while mumbling 'daylight robbery'. He started walking away from me, and then turned. 'You and me should go out for a drink sometime. I can teach you a few things about this miserable world.' I nodded and smiled as enthusiastically as I could.

Off he went out of the door and into the drizzling rain grabbing frantically inside his tattered overcoat for his cigarettes and matches. The cashier gave me a knowing look as I handed over my money. 'Sad to see some people get like that ain't it?' she said. 'Whenever I asks 'im, "How are you luv?" he says, "Mustn't grumble," but of course that's what 'e does all the time. Must be lonely for 'im not being able to trust no one. Sad.'

I walked back to the office. It was time to look a bit deeper into this trust thing. If we sometimes don't trust each other when working in the same office, how much more difficult is it when we're thousands of miles apart?

JUST SAY NO

Got a call this afternoon from Paula's allergist. Paula had sent her my e-mail about being allergic to alcohol and the resulting pustules. The allergist was fascinated by my condition and offered to see me free of charge. I politely declined saying that it was really hard for me to get out because of the increasing pollutants in the London air. I had to work at home more and more. 'Wear a face mask,' she said. I replied that I couldn't do that because I was allergic to the material. She said she would come and visit me which I parried with, 'I'm afraid my father has only just been let out of hospital and is recovering from that awful skin-eating bacteria.' Lies, lies, and more lies spiralling into absurdity when all I really had to say was, 'No, thank you.'

ON CAMERA

I had an e-mail from Parker Bagley, a fellow classmate from the MBA programme in New York: *Will. Just read that Britain is now **the** surveillance society. You've got 1 CCTV camera over there for every 14 people.*[5] *Made any impact on you, personally?*

I replied: *yes, I dress better when I go out.*

SO MANY HITS, SO LITTLE TIME

Before I tell you about my Google results on trust, I found it funny that when I typed 'Google' into my notes I got a red line underneath it as though I'd misspelled the name.

---

[5] Finding of a Surveillance Studies Network report and reported on the BBC News website, 2 November 2006.

When I went into Tools: Spelling and Grammar, I got a number of alternatives – Goggle, Go ogle, Goggles, Gouge, Goggled, and Googol. You'd think by now that the computer dictionary would have caught up with Google!

Moving on, my search on 'virtual team trust' yielded a ton of stuff – 17 900 000 hits! I've had to give myself a limit on these open-ended searches. If I don't find the kind of thing I need in the first three to five pages I quit, revise the search terms, or decide the search wasn't worth doing in the first place. My father says I'm part of the 'Give me what I want, when I want it, how I want it, and where I want it' generation. I'm not sure what his point is! Isn't this progress? Instant knowledge that you don't have to think about too much!

After a morning trawling through websites, the first thing I did was to create a working definition of virtual trust: the confidence you have that team colleagues who work with you primarily via technology can be relied upon – despite challenges such as distances, different time zones, and cultures – to meet or exceed expectations in working towards shared goals. Not bad. Afterwards I went into the GO*dz*W*illa* applications and created a mind map. (see facing page)

Let me explain some of this for you. In trying to make sense of all that I found, four major pathways emerged: Mindset, Context, Behaviours, and Process.

1. Mindset. In here I've put nine personal qualities that help develop a climate for virtual trust. I think most of them are self-explanatory, but let me describe a couple. 'Caring' can seem out of place in business, but when you're working virtually it's good to know that others are thinking about how you are doing, that you're not just an e-mail address. 'Reciprocity' is not an urban school for chefs (joke!), but the critical give and take so necessary on effective teams. These personal qualities are important for the success of any team, but on a virtual team they need not just to be present but felt to be present. Distance can dilute and distort good

Thinking about virtual trust.

intentions, so we need to make extra efforts to make them real.

2. Context. This is knowledge of the circumstances that can impact trust on the team. If the complexity of the task is high and the risk level is high, it might be difficult to build trust until the competence and reliability of other team members has been demonstrated. Also, what awareness do team members have about themselves and each other, and the contribution each one can make to the success of the team? What awareness of differences in style and personality is there, and of how they can complement one another? Finally, there are the challenges whose impact might need to be minimized – a changing and uncertain business environment; a fragmented organization with dysfunctional internal competition; incompatible technological platforms; different processes and methods; time zone and cultural differences.

3. Behaviours. These are the everyday actions members need to demonstrate if trust is to live and prosper. I've divided them into two paths: Giving Trust and Getting Trust. All of the behaviours are important, but let me highlight a few.

'Suspending doubt about trustworthiness' – you need to assume at the beginning that everyone is trustworthy and has the interests of the team at heart. This may turn out not to be the case, but if you assume trustworthiness upfront you will have done your part in launching the team in a positive way. Start with cynicism and you'll end with cynicism.

'Being present and accessible to everyone' – how can you be trusted if you're not really 'there'? You've got to be visible and available (or at least others need to know when you're available).

'Responding quickly and thoughtfully' – team members need to know you're paying attention and not just going through a routine of responding; just saying 'Good job' or 'Well done' after someone has sent you something they've spent a great deal of time and effort working on leaves them wondering if you have looked at it at all.

'Communicating even when you don't have to' – if you only communicate with someone when you want something from them, the relationship is purely transactional and shallow. In times of difficulty, when a team really needs to pull together, shallow relationships will probably not hold up. Assigning blame, political game playing, competitiveness, withdrawal, and 'got you' games are likely to increase. More communication and greater spontaneity at the beginning is good for creating a foundation.

4. Process. In this pathway I am referring to the need to pay attention to the ongoing developmental stages of the team, and what factors should be emphasized at each stage if trust is to be established and to grow.

In the Forming stage, for example, you must work on establishing the relationships and then move smoothly into the task. It's always a fine balance. Too much time on relationship building upfront can leave the team feeling good about each other, but less good about what they are supposed to be doing. Too much time spent on the task might leave the team clear about what they are doing, but unsure about each other.

There is usually a Transitioning stage for teams when members are bumping up against one another and friction occurs. If relationships have been built then negotiations about what, why, who, how, where, and when should be relatively painless.

The Developing stage is all about the ongoing nurturing of trust to enable it to grow and strengthen. How does this happen? Continuous communication, team interaction, and deeper learning about each other's qualities and capabilities help. There must also be ongoing mutual support, and the recognition and celebration of team successes.

I don't like to boast (or bring-and-brag as my American friends call it), but I thought the map was a pretty clear and concise way of capturing most of the key issues. Spinks saw it printed out on my desktop and couldn't help himself.

'Good effort,' he said, like the condescending (censored) he is. 'Perhaps one day you'll have time to fill in the gaps.'

'Thank you for your astute and welcome observation,' I answered. 'Perhaps you could point out where they are for me. I'd be most grateful.'

'No, no,' he said, 'I'm the last person on earth to interfere and step on someone else's toes. You carry on. Wouldn't want to take the credit away from you.'

If there is a God, why would he, she, or it take the time to create a creature like Spinks?

IS LOVE JUST A CLICK AWAY?

Last night I checked my e-mail before going to bed; there were three responses to my LoveNest.com profile. Brilliant! Life is good! The grammar and spelling mistakes on the first profile turned me off ('I lives in Lundun with tu gnats – Binj and Purrge' – I took the latter to mean 'two cats named Binge and Purge', but who knows?). The reference in the second profile to the astounding genius of John Grisham also put me off. The third – code named 'Beauty for the Beast' – looked like she had great potential: loves hot Indian curries with a glass of beer; likes to travel (had just returned from Egypt); enjoys music (except opera and musicals); is passionate about films (especially action/adventure); reads the classics non-stop; loves Chinese acrobats, digital photography, art (visiting the Tate Modern); and, most importantly, appreciates a great sense of humour. I sent an immediate reply asking if we could e-mail and maybe work up to chatting online.

I TRUST YOU BECAUSE

One night after work I met with a couple of old friends from university – Peter Saylor and Tim Arnold. After graduating, they both went into the financial industry as investment bankers. Sitting in a pub near St Paul's Cathedral we talked about the old days – the parties, the hangovers, the girl-friends. At one point we started talking about trust at work, and some of their stories got me thinking about the whole issue of self-awareness and self-management.

Pete told the story of one of his managers who wouldn't hire anyone who wore brown shoes to an interview. Apparently, the decision to wear brown shoes showed a lack of professionalism!

Pete's story set off Tim who had others to tell. One of his managers would call the interviewee's home phone to listen to the telephone message. If the message were unorthodox in anyway, he or she wouldn't be hired. Another manager of Tim's – if the candidate were male – would take him to a strip club to see how he responded. Did he treat the women at the club with respect? Did he become loutish? What did he reveal about himself in such an environment? Might the manager have had his own agenda?

There are, of course, many reasons why we would choose to trust a person, and this is where self-awareness and self-management come in. Are we able to look objectively at others – and ourselves – and make reasoned choices, or are we puppets strung along by our own unexamined biases?

As I returned home on the underground listening to the wondrous *Alanis Morissette* on my iPod, I made a list of some potential influences on whether or not to trust someone, and if those influences could be considered Good, Neutral, or Bad:

Good	Neutral	Bad
• Demonstrated competence • Demonstrated sense of commitment • Personal experience of the person's trustworthiness	• Third-party perceptions • Individual has a personal stake (e.g. reward) in achieving a successful outcome • Risk to an individual if a successful outcome is not achieved • Person's confidence in themselves	• Accent and other aspects of communication style • Anything to do with a person's race, ethnicity, or culture • Similarity to oneself • Someone's current role

Many other influences could be added – like BROWN SHOES! – but there's not enough memory on my smart phone to list all the quirks people have in deciding whether or not to trust someone. One of the things I learned when doing my BA in Economics and International Relations was that during the Cold War the American policy was TBV (Trust, But Verify). Sounds wise for working virtually.

As I left the Underground station, someone came up behind me, knocked me down, and ran off with my iPod. All I saw was a hooded sweatshirt and a pair of torn jeans disappearing into the darkness of the local park – a nasty RW moment, and I feel naked without my Pod.

BEAUTY AND THE BEAST

For several days now, I've been exchanging e-mails and chatting with 'Beauty for the Beast'. She directed me to a profile on *MySpace*, and so I believe her name is Sophie James. I've actually chatted with her online, and she appears to be real and not a phantom – you know, a phony profile that ends up being an ad for itch cream.

After looking at our *MySpace* profiles, we chatted for hours. We decided to ask each other some questions. There were the usual suspects like: What is your favorite colour, movie, book, or food? The ones I remember best were:

Question	Sophie	Me
What would you do if you could be invisible for a day?	(The above – Ha ha)	Ride a motorbike naked through a tea party at Buckingham Palace
What really annoys you?	Arrogance and ignorance – dangerous combo People who act as if no one else existed People blind to their own failings	When technology doesn't do what it's supposed to do! I want to smash things Pompous asses, hypocrites Anyone who can't laugh at themselves

Question	Sophie	Me
What are your favourite possessions?	China teacup that belonged to my great, great grandmother Handwritten poem given to me by my younger brother	My new iPod, laptop, and mobile phone
If your house caught fire, what things would you grab first?	My boxer dogs; Zeus and Nick the Neurotic Family photos	My new mega-memory iPod, laptop, and mobile phone
What superpower would you like to have?	Only one?? Be able to teleport Be able to walk on the seabed	Ability to absorb the powers of others
If you could change one thing about yourself, what would it be?	Be less shy around others; be more of an extrovert	Get better abs
What is the most difficult thing you have ever had to do?	Cope with my younger brother's suicide when I was eighteen; he was seventeen	Study when I could have been playing online

It should be clear from the above that Sophie is a more thoughtful and sensitive person than I am. I tend to surf on the waves of life while she swims (or walks) in the ocean. I was giving relatively glib answers, but when she revealed what had happened to her brother it was like a hammer blow. I was shocked back into the *real*; her disclosure destroyed any gap that virtual space put between us. I was suddenly and brutally in her world.

Sophie and I both had the sneaking suspicion we had 'met' before in the *Second Life* virtual world. In swapping stories about our experiences in *Second Life*, we both remembered an 'incident' in a bar. It's weird to think we might have been 'quite friendly' for a short time in another world. We might have been even friendlier except that – if I remember correctly – I was totally distracted by a popup saying I'd won an iPhone (which was a lie). That continuous partial attention can be a curse!

While we were answering each other's questions I couldn't help but think that this would be a great way for team members to get to know each other quickly. It would be relatively easy to create an *Electronic Who's Who* of team members. It would be voluntary and wouldn't need to be sophisticated.

SUCKED INTO THE UNNATURAL DISASTER THAT IS BINKS

I heard Geoff Dyson (Diceman), the chief game designer, was making one of his rare appearances in the office, so I went into the Calendar Room on GO*dz*W*illa* and arranged a meeting with him for the afternoon.

Unfortunately, I had to spend the morning meeting with Corbishly Binks (no relation to Spinks although they are often spoken of in the same breath as Binks & Spinks, or more concisely as just BS). Binks is Communications Director even though he is best known for his inability to communicate with anyone inside *The Fun House*. Here's something he wrote for a business paper recently:

> *The Fun House is repurposing its core competencies for transitioning to a position in alignment with market vectors. Leveraging intangible assets horizontally across the extended enterprise enables increased knowledge generation and synergy utilisation.*

Unfortunately, not enough people say 'Stop, or I'll Shoot' when Binks is spitting up his jargon. No, we let such mindless drivel wash over us and pollute the lingosphere – sorry, language! It's a great substitute for thought. I find we're particularly reluctant to challenge Binks on teleconferences because we don't want to prolong being on the phone with him. We assume that the meaning will become clear at some point or that we can turn to one of the other team members for a translation (but usually they don't understand either).

Binks trapped me for a couple hours, and his dizzying whirlpool of incomprehension sucked the life out of me. Face-to-face or virtual, corporate-speak is a communication black hole allowing little meaning to escape its gravitational pull. There's enough distance between people these days, and we don't need to add more through vague, incomprehensible language. We just waste time second-guessing what is really meant, and it builds walls rather than trust.

MEETING WITH THE DICEMAN

After lunch, I headed upstairs to where the Diceman had a workroom for when he is in the office. Inside, I was stunned to find a pair of legs and feet waving at me from behind a desk.

'Hey Will. Glad we're finally able to connect,' said a voice. 'Don't mind me. Yoga. Always stand on my head when needing creativity. Blood to the brain. Grab a chair or stand on your own head if you prefer.'

I sat down on a chair and stared at his sockless, bony, and none-too-clean feet as they peered at me from across the table.

'SHE's asked you to fill her in on the new workplace,' said the voice.

'That's right,' I said feeling somewhat disoriented (I'm having my first face-to-feet meeting, I thought).

'I think SHE does a lot of the right stuff intuitively,' the voice went on.

'What exactly?' I asked.

The feet tilted slightly to the right and up as though they were looking for inspiration. Then they tilted left and down as though thinking. *Note to self: ask Bess if neurolinguistic programming has meanings associated feet movements, not just eyes.*

'One thing you'll learn about SHE,' said the feet, 'is that she believes if you get the right mindset, the results will follow.'

'And what's the right mindset?'

'I think she'd describe it as simple goodwill, acting together in good faith, staying transparent, and being very explicit about what you're thinking and doing. And no psychological or political game playing, but always showing respect, assuming professionalism, and showing how mutual support works for the good of the team.' I encouraged him to keep talking.

'Well, SHE was confident, but not arrogant, she never rushed to judgement, and no matter what the situation was, she always remained calm and pragmatic. Right from the very beginning we all felt this was someone we could trust, even though most of us didn't meet with her face-to-face until much later.'

'Anything else?' I asked.

'Well, she established open and regular communications very early. She didn't leave us guessing about what she expected. She made her presence felt from the very beginning, and she's kept it up. You always feel that there's a leader in the network who is clear, confident, and responsive; someone who has your interests as well as her own in the mix. I'm not saying she tried to wield the 8000 mile screwdriver. ...'

'Sorry, that went right over my head,' I said.

'Oh, right,' said Diceman. 'I hear the Pentagon compares micromanaging across distances – which she chose not to do – to an attempt to tighten a screw with an 8000 mile screwdriver. It can't be done. You can set a strategic direction and negotiate guidelines and expectations, but the rest is communication and trust.'

'So, she created a good climate for trust?' I said.

'Absolutely. I think she modelled early on how she wanted the team to interact.'

'You've given me a few words describing her style – clear, confident, and responsive – any others?' I asked.

'Let's see,' he said, his feet looking pensive. How his feet did that I'm not sure, but they did! He could, I've no doubt, put on a tremendous *Cirque du Soleil* show with just his feet. Eventually he said, 'Warmth, that's another word I would add. Whether you're in the real world or the virtual world,' he continued, 'there are people who are Cold communicators, Warm communicators, and Hot communicators. You know the cold ones – "Hello, knock, knock, is there a human being in there I can speak to? Hello." There's no smile in the voice. It's hard to trust the cold ones because they freeze you out and don't seem to engage. The hot ones, well, I'd divide them into Cheerleaders and Battlers. The *rah rah* cheerleaders want you to feel that everything is fantastic, brilliant; we can be anyone and do anything as long as we believe and put our minds to it. The Battlers are fiery, emotive warriors. Nothing is ever good enough. We're not being smart enough, quick enough, or aggressive enough. We've got to put some fire in our bellies.

'The Warm ones get a good balance – friendly, approachable, responsive, congenial, constructive, but also straight and assertive. There's also a sense of solidarity. SHE makes us feel we're all in this together, and if SHE makes a promise, she keeps it.'

'So you're a big fan of SHE.'

'Of course, who isn't? I'd ask her to come live with me on my houseboat and have my children if she'd have me.'

'She won't?'

'I'm too much of an anarchist, and her being gay of course.'

'SHE … is … gay?' I said.

'Holy Karl Marx. I thought everyone knew,' he gasped as he crumpled to the floor. He lifted himself so that he was kneeling behind the table with his arms wrapped around his head. 'I can't believe I just did that. Too much blood to the brain. Oh man, SHE'll kill me. What have I done?'

'Listen Geoff, she won't have to kill you because I'm not a gossip-monger. What was said in this room, stays in this room. If she wants to tell me sometime, that's fine. SHE is a terrific person, gay, straight, or anywhere in between.'

'Yes, but that was such a crazy stupid thing to do. Oh god.'

'Well, OK, I'll give you that, but. …'

'Can I really trust you with this? I haven't even met you before!'

'Well you've no choice, unless you intend to murder me, which I don't think you will. I haven't betrayed anyone since I told my parents that my sister was smoking an illegal substance behind the garden shed with her school friends. It turned out to be grass cuttings from our lawn.'

'Thanks man. I appreciate that. Oh Jeez!'

BEAUTY SEES THE BEAST

In one of our chats, Sophie and I dared each other to send through photos. The problem was who would send their photo first. We couldn't toss a coin because there was no way of knowing if the person tossing the coin was cheating or not. Eventually we decided it would be the first person who could answer a stupid question, via the Net. The problem was finding a question that neither one of us knew the answer to already. What we did was to agree that after the count of three we would both type a single word in the chat box. She wrote 'Armadillo' and I wrote 'Leprosy', so the question became 'Can armadillos catch leprosy?' The race was on. Within a minute she had the answer, or at least an answer of 'Yes'. She had simply Googled 'Weird Stuff' and found it through a site specializing in crazy facts. I wasn't sure the site could be trusted, but she reminded me that the challenge had been to come up with an answer. Whether the answer was true or not was another question.

I lost so I sent through a picture of myself. The chatting stopped for a while; the suspense was killing me. 'Well?' I typed. 'Patience', she typed backed. After what seemed a geological age, she typed, 'It's a good thing I'm not into looks!' What! My hopes for a soul mate crashed and burned. Then up on the screen came, 'Just joking. I've seen worse! My connection was slow, so it took forever to download your picture. You look how you described yourself, although I think you undersold yourself a bit. You're not half bad. LOL'

'OK, now it's your turn,' I wrote.

'Nah. Maybe, I should sign off now,' she wrote back. 'There's a full moon and I. ...'

'NOOOOOOOOO. You can't do that to me. We had a deal.'

'O alright. Hold on.'

Again the waiting. Come on, come on. Here ... no ... come on, come on! All the big questions about the meaning of life, God, and the universe seemed to fuse into one – do I have enough bandwidth? Yes. Here it is!

O, O, O. ... She was beautiful. ... OK, not in a super-model kind of way with a wasted face, pouty lips, and a touch-me-and-you'll-get-bone-splinters-body. No, Sophie was real, not manufactured to fit someone's twisted template of beauty.

'Well?' she typed.

'I don't know what to say,' I typed back.

'Hmm. That bad.'

'No, no. I'm ... would *you* really want to meet *me*?'

'I'm willing if you are.'

'You mean it?'

'Yes, of course. You seem like an OK person, although perhaps lacking in a bit of self-confidence.'

'Right then. I'll call your mobile Friday night and we'll meet up at an Indian restaurant, somewhere central,' I wrote.

'OK, and we'll continue our little soap opera face-to-face.'

'Hey, don't knock soap opera,' I typed. 'It's today's highest art form, after reality TV.'

'Bye Will. Sleep well.'

Sleep! I wasn't going to go to sleep. How could I sleep?

When we went offline, I thought that photographs would be a good addition to a team's *Electronic Who's Who* – anything to help team members truly appreciate that there is a live human being at the other end of the connection. Wait, hadn't Paula said something similar at our breakfast? The room suddenly turned cold.

But there is a point here. I think. There's so much information and noise in this digital ocean we're swimming in, it's hard to keep track of who says what. Did you say that, did I say that, did I hear it from someone else? Is anything new or are we just synthesizing, mimicking, regurgitating, and re-packaging? There is so much pressure to produce, but what? A copy of a copy of a copy? Hold on tiger, too deep.

AN ALL TOO REAL ENCOUNTER OF A PAINFUL KIND

Late afternoon I was staring out of the window at the illuminated London skyline on the north bank of the Thames. I felt a tap on my shoulder and turned. It was Ruth Wilson, Global Marketing Director.

'Ruth, hi. I'm just looking for inspiration out there.'

'I much prefer cities at night,' she said in a dreamy way, 'especially London and New York. It's been a hell of a day. Fancy a drink before I face Davian.'

'Davian?'

'My four-year-old, named after his two grandfathers, Dave and Ian. His grandmother – poor thing – is taking care of him until about half past seven, so I could in theory clink a glass of something with you before heading home.'

'Right! Excellent. I can pick your brain if that's OK. Why don't we head over to *Happy Sally's*?'

Happy Sally's wine bar attracts investment bankers from across the river, drama lovers heading to the new Globe Theatre, and young office workers in search of – let's be honest – sex. Quite a number of *Fun House* people go there to wind down and complain about something or someone, so much so we often call it the Whine Bar!

We sat in a corner with a couple of glasses of a dry red wine, *Cantina Zaccagnini*, from Abruzzo in Italy. Dark, fruity, mellow, and cheap; it went down very easily although I'm more of a Belgian beer man.

Ruth told me about her family – husband Wallace, a commercial artist and part-time guitarist in a pub band. They're called *Lick Knuckle and the Resisting Fruit.* Apparently the bandleader had gone to a Band Name Generator site on the web and this was the first name that came up. Trusting in the wisdom of the web, he adopted it. They couldn't play very well and only knew three songs, but the name was getting them bookings. Davian was Ruth and Wallace's only child, and was likely to remain so.

'Like I said in the office, is it OK if I pick your brain?' I asked.

'Odd expression isn't it, pick your brain?' Ruth said. 'Something our adorable son might take literally one day; we already hide the knives and forks from him. But anyway, pick away.'

'Right now,' I said, 'I'm thinking about cooperation and trust in the new workplace. Any thoughts?'

'OK. Let me think. … You know when we communicate – whether it's face-to-face or virtual – we each try to convey an impression of who we are and who we're not. We're all in marketing, you know; we're all selling our own brand these days. You, me, we're all expressing something about ourselves consciously and unconsciously all the time. Why do we do it? Age-old reasons like seeking power, being attractive to others, seeking gain, wanting respect.'

'I'm not really into power, gain, or even respect, but I relate to wanting to appear attractive,' I said, while grinning.

'Will, are you fishing for compliments you poor insecure thing?'

'No, nothing like that, but unconsciously, who knows?'

'As I was saying,' Ruth went on, 'when you're virtual, you work at giving an impression to your colleagues either in e-mails, web meetings, or video conferencing. You want to be seen as the person you want them to believe you are, if that makes any sense.'

'Who do you want to be?' I asked.

'Me? I like others to see me as professional, confident, intelligent, honest, in control of myself, respectful, tolerant, and easy to get along with. Not the panicked mother of a four-year-old delinquent, who is also incredibly cranky first thing in the morning, and who is being driven to even greater heights of crankiness by incurable Athlete's Foot.

'Other people don't have any clues about you other than the ones you convey through the technology. People build a picture of you based on very little information, and this image tends to be idealized, which might be for the best. Does a virtual colleague really need to know your inner demons and anxieties? I know personal boundaries seem to be out of fashion, but knowing that I can be really cranky, that I can be amazingly sarcastic, and that my Athlete's Foot is giving me hell doesn't help or hinder the virtual relationship. I think that in the virtual world we each need to take responsibility for constructing and maintaining a persona that helps to build trust and collaboration.'

'Wait a minute,' I said, 'you mean we should build trust on a lie, a persona, and not our real selves?'

'What would your *real* self be, Will? And, if you were to find such a thing would it help or hinder the collaboration?'

'But a persona is a fiction, it's not real.'

'What did you study at University?' she said, 'before business.'

'Economics and International Relations.'

'I see. So you're clueless about the power of fiction to convey reality,' she said. 'Most of the time fact is fiction dressed up as fact,' she went on, obviously enthused by the topic. 'Look, I'm not saying that we should all create personas that are 180 degrees from our habitual ones. Everyday life is a whole series of personal performances in different situations. I don't act in the same way with my husband as I do with my gynecologist. I adapt, and I want to see people coming into the virtual workplace wearing a persona that will be productive for the whole team.'

'But don't we want people to be themselves, to be authentic?' I argued.

'Nooooooo. I think that's the last thing we want,' she said. 'The world is full of authentic idiots who screw things up by being themselves all the time. I don't want to see more "authentics" spilling their dysfunctional guts all over the virtual stage. Give me a lie that works rather than a reality that doesn't.'

'I see one problem with what you're saying,' I said boldly. 'In my experience, which granted isn't huge, I've seen people get really mad when the virtual person they thought they knew turns out differently; they feel betrayed and sometimes stupid.'

'That's true,' she said. 'But the real issue is productive self-management and not authenticity. It's just so complicated these days,' she went on. 'In this so-called digital age we can be as many public selves as we want. And who's to say which one is the real one? This is the Age of Proteus,[6] you know, the shape-shifter.'

'OK. Anything else you'd like to reveal beyond your early morning crankiness and Athlete's Foot?' I asked with a smile.

Ruth reminded me that she had to leave and pick up Davian from her mother's before irreparable damage was

---

[6] Proteus – Sea god in Greek myth famous for his ability to change form, e.g. become water, a tree, a leopard.

done to property or relationships. We finished our glasses of wine and stood up to leave.

'Don't leave on my account, you ape,' said a voice behind me. 'Allergic to alcohol are you, you lying, two-faced, jerk.'

It was Paula. Oh lord, save me. 'Paula, nice to see you again, let me introduce. ...'

'I want no introductions from you, you rat. I see you obviously go for the older, frumpier type. Searching the female species for another mother are you?' Paula's face was aflame and her breath between outbursts was a panting fury.

With eyes agog, every head in the wine bar had turned in our direction. I was acutely aware of the smirking masses all around me. My pulse pounded like an elephant tap dancing as I tried to think of a way out. Ruth looked at me, puzzled.

'Paula, perhaps we could talk about this outside,' I said as calmly as I could.

'Oh no, chicken-heart, you don't escape that easily,' she hissed.

'But Paula, I hardly know. ...'

The stab Paula gave my right foot with her stiletto zapped every nerve in my body with electric howls of pain. I fell back into my chair gasping for air while Paula storm-troopered her way out of the bar to the cheers and applause of the mob. So much for the so-called wisdom of crowds!

The manager asked if I would like to call the police, but I managed to mouth a 'no thank you'. The last thing I wanted was further contact with Paula.

'Drink this,' said Ruth holding a large brandy. 'No wait, I need this and you need a taxi. By the way, was that enough authenticity for you?'

CONVERGENCE

DANCE YOUR OWN DANCE

Received an SMS[7] on my phone from a lonely-hearts group that has found me, probably through LoveNest.com. I've been invited to a dance opposite platform nine at Waterloo Station. Apparently this is called 'mobile clubbing' – bring music that you want to dance to on your iPod. Everybody can be dancing to different music, it doesn't matter. Might as well give it a try.

DID YOU DO THAT ON PURPOSE?

'Did you do that on purpose?' my mother used to say when I'd done damage to something or someone – like cracking the glass in the new kitchen skylight with a hit-for-six cricket ball or dislodging two of my sister's teeth with a magic-powered Viking sword (actually a small branch from a neighbour's apple tree). My answer, of course, was always, 'No, I didn't. Sorry.' I got away with lots of stuff as long as it wasn't *on purpose*. Now, as an adult, everyone is telling me I *need* a purpose. Yesterday I received a letter from my father asking me if I'd figured out what I was going to do with my life. My father – Gareth – is a retired history teacher who periodically gets in touch by snail mail while he's travelling around Britain in an old Ford Transit van converted into a

---

[7] Short Message Service – text messaging.

camper. He says he's writing the definitive guide to Roman ruins, although I think he's just trying to escape from my Thespian mother, Beverly. He doesn't consider my working in a computer games company as a noble purpose. My sister also (perhaps in revenge for the dislodged teeth incident) is always sending me questionnaires to discover my true purpose. What if my purpose is to be purpose-free? What if I want to be 'content-free' and 'outcome-neutral', but have a good time along the way?

Sunil had included 'Convergence' as a performance zone for global virtual teams and so I knew I had to spend some time wrestling with the dreaded 'purpose' gremlin, at least from a team point of view. I can probably handle it without too much soul-searching. On a recent call I asked him why he had included Convergence in his model.

'Because William, without an engaging and clear purpose a team can easily lose its bearings. You're English so you probably like the game of football,' he said.

'Yes, Liverpool's my team,' I said proudly.

'Manchester United is mine,' he said, 'but that's beside the point. Have you ever seen a team that seems to have forgotten that the inherent purpose of the game is to put the ball between the opponent's goal posts? Some teams seem to think the purpose is to just keep possession of the ball longer than the other team. Possessing the ball for 99 percent of the time doesn't win you the game. Your opponents can still win if they score during their miniscule 1 percent. And another thing, the players really need to understand the purpose fully before they go on to the pitch; they shouldn't be discovering it during the game!'

'True,' I said.

'It's the same in global virtual teamwork. We spend time thinking about "who", "how", and "when", but often little on "why". The other questions are important, don't get me wrong, but if we forget that the purpose is to put the ball in the back of our opponent's goal, all of our hard work will count for very little, if anything.

'I'd like to see our group as a purpose-built and purpose-driven team that stays on-purpose,' he said. 'That kind of team can often beat ones with more skillful players and more resources.'

'We do have GO*dz*W*illa* to help keep us on track,' I offered.

'That's true William, but that's the pitch we play on, it isn't our purpose. But don't get me wrong, it is a very fine pitch.'

'Thanks Sunil. It's always a pleasure talking to you, even if you are a Manchester United supporter,' I said.

'And one day you might see the light, William,' he replied laughing.

SOMETHING MISSING

This afternoon I went into GO*dz*W*illa* and joined the senior team weekly video web meeting. After a few minutes of free-form jabber, SHE asked us to go into REVERSE. This was simply the part of the meeting when the Global Functional Heads and the Regional Heads gave us the highlights from their previous week's reports. The reports had been posted on the web before the meeting so the Heads didn't need to present too much detail. With this group of hyperactives and multitaskers, presenting needed to be kept to an absolute minimum, and the emphasis placed on questions, feedback, and discussion. Most of the time, we tend to use web meetings for same-time collaboration rather than one-to-many presentations.

The next phase of the meeting was what SHE called – you've guessed it – FORWARD. This phase was divided into several 'gears' (perhaps I should have mentioned that SHE is a fan of car racing; in fact, she has been known to compete in rallies in her supercharged Mini Cooper). Anyway, First Gear was devoted to discussing items that absolutely must be done in the coming week. Second Gear was for those critical items just over the horizon, i.e. the following weeks and months. Third Gear was focused on those items that were important over the longer term, e.g. trends in the marketplace. Third Gear items would shift over time into Second and First Gears.

The end of the meeting was devoted to PARKING. This was where SHE asked us to 'park' a thought in everyone's head for the coming week. Some tried to be inspirational, others were cynical, and some were Zen-like ('My empty cup is overflowing with silence'). Other thoughts just relayed something in the news that had captured their attention, like the individual on the transatlantic flight who had flushed the toilet while still sitting on it, causing a vacuum to form in the bowl. This resulted in the said individual having to be levered off the seat by workmen at Heathrow! *Note to self: working virtually has more benefits than I ever imagined.*

Overall the meeting was efficient, productive, and fun. The structure was clear and logical, everyone contributed, and there were actual outcomes. But something was nagging at me about the meeting, something I couldn't quite put my finger on.

THE MYSTERY ALLIANCE

I've been asking around about the Anglo-Saxon Alliance Spinks is working on, but no one seems to know anything about it. People are beginning to wonder if Spinks might have started his own fantasy game business on the side.

I did have a disturbing conversation with him this morning as I made love to my Caffeine Tornado.

'I hear that you did an MBA in America,' he said rather curtly.

'That's right, in New York.'

'I see,' he pomped (that's what I've decided to call his way of talking – he pomps).

'What's wrong with our British business schools, or couldn't you get into one?'

I was a bit taken aback. 'Well ... I like experiencing other places, getting a different perspective, and New York sounded exciting. I suppose I'm a bit of a global citizen ...'

'Global citizen! Don't be ridiculous. That's being a citizen of nowhere. You're British for God's sake.'

'Well yes, that's what my passport says, and I'm perfectly happy being British, but there's a big world out there to get to know.'

'Most of it unfortunately is finding its way in here, and no I don't wish to get to know it thank you very much.'

I didn't want to get into an argument with Spinks so I smiled and pretended there was an urgent call I had to make to a software group in South East Asia.

He was gibbering something about a Third World take-over as he wandered off to find someone from Maintenance. They hadn't come to fix his desk lamp and he found that 'Just infuriatingly negligent!'

WE DON'T KNOW WHERE WE ARE GOING, BUT WE'RE MAKING GOOD TIME

The day after the teleconference I decided to call Ruth Wilson. I saw from GO*dz*W*illa* that Ruth was working from home. Perhaps she could help me pinpoint what had been nagging me about the meeting.

'Hello Ruth, this is Will.'

'Hi Will. How's your poor foot?'

'Horrible colours and scabby.'

'Whooo, sorry. Anyway, Will, what's up?' I could hear the piercing yells of a youngster in the background, as well as what sounded like a Rottweiler having its ears pulled off.

'Is this a good time?' I asked sheepishly.

'Sure. Why do you ask?' she said.

Ruth seemed oblivious to the canine cries for help, so I carried on. 'I just wanted to chat about the team meeting we had yesterday. Was it fairly typical?'

'Yes, I think so. Why?'

'Even though it was a good meeting, I couldn't help but feel something was missing.'

'You mean like virtual office politics? All of the negative game playing that people know is there, but nobody wants to talk about?'

'Really?'

'Of course! We're all human beings. There are times when conflicts arise about the task or the process, available resources or even behaviour, but we try to keep it open and constructive. If it's a relationship or personality issue, SHE puts the responsibility for solving it on those involved, unless there is absolute deadlock. She'll only step in as a last resort.'

'No, I don't think that's it, although I would like to hear more about that sometime. I feel it had more to do with some of the team not seeing the bigger picture.'

'Ah, OK. I think you're right, and I know it's something SHE wants to fix,' Ruth said.

'So what's missing exactly?'

'A clear sense of what we're all about and an overall strategy shared by the team. You see, Will, this team existed before SHE came along, and it came together in the heady entrepreneurial days of Art Kelly. Back then the games tended to sell themselves, but now there are many more competitors out there and they are aggressive and well organized.'

'But everyone seemed pretty aligned with each other,' I said.

'Yes, but that's an illusion,' she said amused. 'That's just on the surface of the meeting. One of the first things SHE did when she came in was to set targets for the regions, and even for the global functions. Setting targets was very necessary to create discipline on the team, but targets are not the same thing as sharing a common sense of purpose and direction.'

'Is that so important if you're meeting targets, which everyone seems to be doing?' I said.

'Oh absolutely,' she answered. 'Like any global virtual team it's very hard for us to focus our combined energies. Because of distance and the pressure of the "local", we're very susceptible to what I call *focus drift*. It's very easy for us to become distracted by what's immediate to us and lose sight of what the team is trying to do.'

'So, if you were SHE, what would you do?' I asked.

'Do you know our game *Beast*?' she said.

'Sorry. I haven't ventured into that one yet.'

'You should! It's the winner of a Golden Joystick award! The game takes place in the underground world of Zhon – a many-headed, many-eyed beast that prowls the caverns and corridors of its world looking for human sacrifices to devour. These sacrifices are thrown into Zhon's world by aliens who have colonized Earth.'

'Sounds like my kind of thing,' I said, half jokingly.

'Our team is like Zhon – it's many-headed and many-eyed. On the one hand, that's great! Many different perspectives are brought to the virtual table. On the other hand, we can easily charge off in different directions. If that happens, we simply waste our energies trying to pull the rest of the beast in the direction each one of us wants to go. The advantage Zhon has over us is that it can see what all of its parts are up to. It can then coordinate them in the pursuit of the tastiest humans. It's hard for us to achieve that same cohesion working virtually. We will always have many heads and eyes, but those eyes need to have one line-of-sight towards the goal. Purpose and plans,' she continued. 'If the team has those, they can move forward together with energy, focus, and confidence.'

'That's true for any team, right?'

'Yes. But think of a virtual team as having an exponentially increased chance of drifting off into space. Whatever we do on a virtual team, it's got to be explicit and tangible. No second-guessing. A virtual team needs markers to help it navigate, and purpose and planning provide some of those.'

'You've been very helpful Ruth. Many thanks.'

'No problem Will. See you, and take care.'

The Rottweiler was now silent, and I wanted to ask if it was OK. I could hear the youngster in the background yelling, 'MASTER OF THE UNIVERSE SAYS "SIT!"'

NATURE AND WILL ABHOR A VACUUM

As I was leaving the *Fun House* tonight for the Underground, looking forward to the *Arctic Monkeys* pile-driving into my eardrums, I noticed Spinks with a mini vacuum cleaner sucking up dust from his computer keyboard. After my conversation about where I'd done my MBA, I decided to try and find out a bit more about Spinks.

'I'm doing a personal survey, Shakespeare. Tell me, do you have a purpose in life?'

'Why on earth do you want to know that?'

'It's just that my sister and father are trying to persuade me that I need a *purpose*. What's yours Shakespeare?'

'Simple; cleaning up the messes of globalization. Everything's being turned upside down and inside out. We're losing everything that has made us British and top-notch. Damn shame, and it's not on. Order needs to be re-established.'

'And you're doing this all by yourself?' I asked.

'Of course not! There are many of us who feel the same way.'

'And you're starting the global cleanup with your keyboard, which was probably made in several Asian countries you realize?'

'Ha bloody ha. I hear that you're a funny man Williams. You'll have to demonstrate your wit to me sometime.'

'Tell me one more thing before I go. I'm looking for a fantasy game called Anglo-Saxon Alliance. Have you heard of it?'

His head turned sharply towards me. 'That's for me to know and you to find out,' he said coldly.

MOBILE SNUBBING

The mobile clubbing at Waterloo Station was a bit of a disappointment. I'm pretty sure that if you didn't have the latest iPod with the biggest memory and accessories, you really didn't rate as a *bona fide* member of the human race. I'd also forgotten to keep my iPod charged so I had no music, which didn't help my already dismal dance moves. Everyone dancing to different music – or no music – didn't really matter (unlike a team, I thought later, where dancing to the same music is a bit of a plus). Met no one new and spent a Siberian evening in the railway station café hugging a mug of putrid coffee. The excitement is just too much for me to bear.

DUST BOWL BLUES

This morning I brought in a large envelope full of dust balls from behind my mini fridge. When Spinks went off to get his mid-morning Earl Grey tea, I scattered some of the dust balls over his keyboard. I know it was a childish, moronic thing to do, but some devil inside made me do it. Bess is right! Time to grow up, Will. *Note to self: Google 'maturity' and see if there's a three to five step maturity programme I can complete in a few days.*

When Spinks came back and saw the dust balls on his keyboard, he spent an anxious few minutes looking for holes in the ceiling. He called Maintenance to take a look – they didn't come. Eventually, he took out his mini vacuum cleaner and cleaned up the mess. The mysterious appearance of dust balls on his keyboard occurred twice more that day. The second time prompted more examining of the ceiling and another call to Maintenance – again, they didn't come. The third time dust balls appeared triggered an outburst: 'Now see here, you pathetic excuses-for-men. Whichever one of you juveniles is messing up my desk you'd better watch out. I'm getting really … really frightfully upset about this. I warn you all I've got a black belt in origami.'

'Karate,' I whispered.

'Like I said, a black belt in karate.' He dove into his desk, pulled out his mini vacuum cleaner and waved it threateningly. Of course, no one but me knew what was happening so they looked at him as though he was having a psychotic meltdown.

Moonbeam accused him of being a sexist for automatically assuming it was one of the men in the office that had done … whatever it was. Spinks called Maintenance again and yelled at them for 10 minutes for ignoring his calls. Someone in Maintenance told me later they had hung up on him seconds after he started ranting. His display of bravado was just for us.

HONG KONG CALLING

Sadie walked towards me through the emerald ocean. Her dark body silhouetted against the azure sky. Her sinuous arms reaching out to hold me against her full breasts. Blood pounding against my temples … oh Sadie.

Vwwwwwwwwwwwwwww. Vwwwwwwwwwwwwww. It was my (censored) mobile phone vibrating like a … well, a vibrating phone, on my bedside table. The painfully neon alarm clock said 03:30. You've got to be (censored) joking!

'Yes,' I rasped.

'Hello Will. This is Aki Kwon in Hong Kong.'

Aki, I knew, was Head of Market Development in Asia. 'Yes Aki, how can I help?'

'So sorry calling this time, but not sure if early or late for you right now.' Three thirty am – early or late? Interesting question … but not one deserving to be speculated upon at THREE THIRTY in the morning! I hadn't signed on for the 24-hour shift or was that the only shift there was in *The Fun House*?

'I am leaving on remote trip for two weeks,' Aki continued, 'and I want make sure I share thoughts about the team. Right now, I in taxi heading for airport. Can you talk?'

'I'm not going anywhere right now,' I said with just a touch of the bitters. 'Let me turn on my laptop and I'll take a few notes.'

Notes from Call with Aki Kwon

- Aki feels that if you talk to different members of the team you'll get different views on priorities. I told her what Sunil and Ruth had said about purpose and planning, and Aki told me that I *must* add priorities.
- There's a problem with shared understanding. For example, there has been some confusion around terms like 'urgent' and 'standardization'. Assumptions are made that everyone shares common interpretations. If we don't question what we think of as the 'obvious', we won't discover differences until it's too late.
- I asked Aki if GO*dz*W*illa* didn't provide the necessary cohesive platform for the team. The answer was an emphatic 'No'. 'No matter how good the collaborative tool,' she said, 'if the team doesn't fully understand what it is doing and why, no amount of technology will save it from going around in circles or meeting numerous dead ends.'

When the call finished, I couldn't get back to sleep. The dream about Sadie had left me overstimulated, but empty (much like my virtual self). I got up and made myself a bacon and fried egg sandwich. My sister says my eating is just a way to fill the inner void created by unmet emotional needs. Whatever. It still tastes out-of-this-world no matter *why* I'm really stuffing it into my face. Sometimes a bacon and egg sandwich is just a bacon and egg sandwich.

SNAKE IN SPANDEX

You won't believe it, but Spinks has had an extreme make-over. For several days now, he's come to the office dressed not in his *Young Farmer Chic* but in neon orange, yellow, and black Spandex. I assumed that he was throwing himself into a fitness programme and riding a bicycle to work; apparently that's not the case. Moonbeam has seen him riding to work on his usual bus. She has also seen him – more than usual – parading up and down outside SHE's office, and occasionally leaning suggestively against the doorframe to ask about her plans for the weekend or her favourite food. Spandex (as everyone knows) holds few secrets from the public gaze. Love is not called a sickness for nothing.

One thought that strikes me is how much I would miss this playing out of the human drama if all of my work was virtual.

WIT'S END

This morning I did what I usually do, went into GO*dz*W*illa* and picked up the news on various sites like the *BBC, CNN, The Guardian, The Times,* and *The New York Times.* I also looked at sites like *Technorati* and *Blogpulse* to see what people are writing about, and I have a few favorite blogs. Of course, I also receive RSS[8] feeds from my aggregators. The problem is I could spend hours getting lost in all of this stuff so I have to scan quickly, and often rely on others who *Digg* items and on *del.icio.us* for what's being tagged.

While I was drinking my CT, I went into *The Wit's End Café* on GO*dz*W*illa.* I saw that Daavid Gustafsson from Helsinki was in there so I opened a chat with him. After initial introductions, I told him what I was working on.

Will: Has Sunil shared the Six Performance Zones with you?
Daavid: Yes, a while ago.

---

[8] Really Simple Syndication – a format for distributing changing online information from sources such as news-related sites and weblogs.

Will: Right now I'm thinking about what Sunil calls the Convergence area. He only talked about Purpose, but since then I've had others add Plans and Priorities. Any thoughts?

Daavid: Let me think for a moment.

He was uncommunicative for quite a while.

Will: Hello Daavid. Still there?

Daavid: Still thinking. Patience ☺

Will: Right. Sorry.

Daavid: This might just be my bias, but I think virtual teams need good performance indicators to help steer them. And as you said, we must also be clear about what our priorities are. *Note to self: Purpose, Priorities, Plans, Performance Indicators. I see a 'P' framework emerging – maybe I should look seriously into management consulting.*

Will: You already have targets don't you?

Daavid: Yes, true, but those are revenue and profitability targets. They don't, for example, tell us how well we are working as a team.

Will: Good point, thanks. Any plans to come and visit us in London?

Daavid: Sorry Will, but I have to close now and meet with SHE.

I looked over at SHE's office and she was sitting there in front of her monitor.

Will: You're having a web meeting?

Daavid: No. I apologize, Will. I'm actually sitting in a cubicle behind you. I'm over here for a couple of days.

Daavid stood up and leaned over the cubicle wall smiling. We shook hands and had a good laugh. 'Maybe we can meet in an RW café for lunch,' he said. 'I'll pay. I owe you.'

SO THAT'S IT!

Moonbeam did the obvious thing and Googled Anglo-Saxon Alliance. It has variations, but in the case of Spinks, it seems pretty clear. It's not a fantasy game, although perhaps you could say it is.

In brief: globalization and immigration have spawned new nationalist movements throughout Europe. In 1980, the New National Front in Britain called for an 'Anglo-Saxon Alliance' of the UK, Germany, and the USA. Today the nationalists want to restore the white make-up of the British population and secure the future of the indigenous people of the islands.

Spinks has obviously swallowed this simplistic philosophy whole. He might be a figure of fun and ridicule in *The Fun House*, but he's committed to a purpose, and I'm beginning to understand the power of purpose – for better or worse. Maybe having Spinks around will help form my own reason for being in the game of life, even if that is just being an antidote to him. Binks, perhaps, is the communications director of this Alliance, in which case we've got absolutely nothing to worry about.

SERIOUS, FOR ONE MOMENT

Daavid and I went to a Greek kebab place for lunch. We both had a *gyro* sandwich that I can never eat without making a mess. The sauce always ends up on the table or in my lap, but it's sooo worth it. I once spent a summer hitchhiking around Greece, and the tastes take me right back to sitting on sun-soaked rocks under olive, pine, and cypress trees staring at the transparent sea.

For some reason, Daavid and I started talking about the games men and women play to draw attention to one another – not an unimportant subject when you're 27 and without a mate. I told him a story from my Greek summer when I was sitting on a boat in Rhodes harbour with some Greek friends. They taught me so much about creativity in the game of life. They were sitting at the stern of the boat next to the harbour wall, and there were many beautiful young women passing by. Try as they might, my friends couldn't entice any of them on board. Suddenly one of my friends opened a toolbox and pulled out a hammer. He jumped off the boat and ran after a stunning girl wearing a bronze tan and little else. When he reached her, he thrust the hammer into her hand, and said, 'Excuse me, you dropped this,' and then he hurried back to the boat. She looked utterly confused for a while, and then walked over to where our boat was tied up.

'You make mistake,' she said softly, handing the hammer back to my friend. 'This not mine.'

'What! I am so, so sorry,' he exclaimed. 'You must think me a complete fool. My name is Barnabas. Please, come aboard and accept a glass of Retsina for your trouble.' And she did!

'See how much we can learn when we are open to other cultures,' said Daavid.

'I'm not sure we can call it cultural,' I laughed, 'but it was enlightening.'

'I've been thinking on what we were chatting about earlier,' Daavid continued in a more serious tone. 'I think the more awareness we have about the games we play with each other the better. The hammer story is an extreme example of one of our games, and no one is going to stop us from making up new games to get what we want.'

'So what are you saying,' I asked. 'I feel like I'm missing something.'

'We all play games, even on our *Fun House* teams. So what I've been thinking about is another piece of Convergence, he said earnestly.'

'OK, if you want to be serious, go on.'

'It's about principles.'

'Oh, really serious!'

'Have you ever been SCUBA diving?' he asked.

'Not yet, but it's on my list of Life's To Dos.'

'I recommend it, but my point is when you're at depth you can lose track of what's up and what's down; you also need to keep your buoyancy, which can be difficult at first. It seems to me that a virtual global team is swimming at depth in an ocean of data and differences. It's easy to lose your sense of direction and your buoyancy, but principles help to keep the team stabilized, along with the other things you've mentioned like purpose. They're all markers in the team's cyber-ocean, letting it know where it is and where it needs to go.'

'What kind of principles?'

'Principles about how we're going to work together.'

'Can you give me some examples?'

'Respect is the first that comes to mind, although we would need to reach some common understanding about what that looks like. Honesty with each other is another one; we shouldn't be hiding things or misleading others.'

'OK. I can see those would be valuable. Any more?'

'Let's go back to talking about your adventures in Greece,' he laughed.

'No. Give me more.'

'How about we agree to keep promises, respect confidentiality, and handle conflict constructively?'

'Good. One more and I'll buy you a Caffeine Tornado.'

'Bribery. OK, I can be bought. Let's see … well, it's important for everyone to accept mutual accountability for results. Everyone must take ownership. Everyone has individual accountabilities, of course, but the team stands and falls together.'

'OK. Thanks Daavid. Let me now walk you to *Has Bean* and the greatest caffeine ride this side of anywhere.'

A NEW FACE

SHE gathered us all together this morning to introduce a new member of the team – Nisha Shenoy. She's going to manage global recruitment during our rapid growth. We all gathered around Nisha to shake her hand and give her a warm welcome, except for Spinks who I saw heading off to the toilets. I liked Nisha immediately. She's the kind of person you feel you've known forever. Her eyes did most of the talking for her. They were serious and playful, open and watchful, dark and bright, but always welcoming.

During our brief introduction, I learned that Nisha was born, raised, and currently living in West London with her extended family. She had two children and was married to a Doctor. I told her about my love of Indian food and she said she would make a Chicken Makani for me some time. That's one Indian dish I haven't tried.

Spinks eventually came out of the toilets and sat at his desk. He looked across at Nisha on the other side of the room then turned to me shaking his head.

'I don't believe it,' he said. 'What the hell is Sheila thinking?'

'I'm not following,' I said.

'Hiring her type.'

'Type?'

'Indian, for God's sake. You can't trust them, and she'll just hire more of her own kind. It's preposterous!'

'I think you'll find she's British,' I said with an edge to my voice.

'Rubbish!' Spinks retorted. 'It takes more than a passport to make someone British.'

When Nisha saw Spinks, she came hurrying over to him.

'You must be Mr Spinks,' she said. 'I've heard so much about you. It's wonderful to finally meet you.' She held out her hand to him and I wondered with some trepidation what Spinks would do next.

He looked at a complete loss and was turning a bright vermilion that out-neoned his Spandex. Slowly, he raised his hand and loosely clasped hers. 'The pleasure's all mine,' he said through semi-clenched teeth.

'We have much to do,' Nisha said to him. 'There's a lot of hiring to be done and I'll be counting on your help with the finances.' She lifted her pleasant, round face and smelled the air. 'That aroma, Earl Grey tea isn't it,' she said excitedly. 'My absolute favourite. I'll bring you in a special blend I get from an Auntie in New Delhi and we can drink some together.'

Off she went, her dark blue sari splashing a brilliant daub of colour in our drab office. Spinks sat looking dazed and confused. This is going to be interesting, I thought to myself.

SOME THINGS MIGHT BE BETTER FACE-TO-FACE

Arriving this morning, I bumped into SHE. We stood outside for a moment while I told her some of my recent findings relating to the workplace project, particularly the criticality of shared purpose and priorities at the global – not just local – level. She smiled.

'It's true,' she said. 'We need to be taking the local blinders off and creating a common view of who we are, where we're going, and how we are going to get there. I think, Will, it would be disastrous for me to try and impose answers to those questions. We really need to do it as a team so that there is shared ownership. I also think this is something we need to do face-to-face over a couple of days. It's very difficult to gain strong commitment unless people are together in one place where they can eat, drink, laugh, hug, and be stupid together. Why don't you look at getting the senior team together early in the New Year for a couple of days. Make it so, Will.'

While we were talking we both saw Spinks getting off a bus dressed-to-impress in his Spandex.

'I've really got to talk to him,' said SHE. 'The mating ritual he's putting on outside my office really belongs on one of those TV nature programmes. If he struts his Bird of Paradise feathers around me one more time, he's going to get plucked.'

SHE, you're my hero! Heroine? Whatever! I can't keep up with what vocabulary is in and what's out.

COORDINATION

IF FOOD BE THE MUSIC OF LOVE, EAT ON

Received a text from Sophie (yes, she has become my seren-ity island in this exhibitionist, hyperstimulated, I-Me-Mine, and terrorized world). She was letting me know that she had read a great review for an Indian restaurant in Soho. Our goal is to try out every Indian restaurant in central London. Now, there's a challenge and a half!

Sophie is also trying to enhance my cultural education, so I find myself going to art galleries and plays with her. She also has me reading the same novels and poetry that she is so we can share our thoughts about them as we scoff our Baltis and Vindaloos. I drew the line at Jane Austen. I try to get the audio versions of the novels and poetry so that I can download them on to my new black and chrome iPod, and listen to them while I'm on the Underground. She says that takes away the pleasure of reading a book, but I don't get that. It's one of the few things I don't get about her. I think I'm falling for this shy, sensitive woman with the big green eyes and dark ringlets. Oh God, she's sure to dump me.

'I think we should both read T.S. Eliot's poem *Burnt Norton* before we meet for our next Indian food fest,' she said in her quiet way. 'There are several lines in there that keep popping into my head, like "Distracted from distraction by distraction". It seems to me to say so much about today's world.'

'That's fine,' I said, 'as long as I can download it quickly from somewhere, and *it* doesn't become a distraction.' Ha!

READY, SET, IMPROVISE

I don't really care if I have children because my sister has two that fill up my world, Emily (Em) and Sebastian (Seb), the Purgatory Twins as I affectionately call them. Why have your own kids when you can have huge amounts of fun with someone else's and none of the exhausting craziness? Em and Seb are like virtual kids – they're real, but not real *here*, not real *right now*, and not real *in my face*. If I had to live with them, I would probably want to sell them, but distance can be priceless. I'm sure if some teams had to work face-to-face the whole time they wouldn't survive as teams.

My sister Bess left me a voice mail on my mob (sorry! mobile) this morning: *Gran's varicose veins are getting worse – or at least more noticeable. Seb saw her in the bathroom this morning and then came to me and said, 'Why is Gran allowed to draw with blue felt pen on her legs and I'm not? S'not fair!'*

Isn't it great to be alive when you can instantly share moments like that? I should explain that Gran is my mother's mother. She lives with Bess, her long-suffering husband Noel, and, of course, the Purgatories. My mother is too busy directing and starring in the latest amateur theatrical extravaganza to take any care of Gran.

Part of my reasoning for not wanting children of my own is that I just don't think I will ever have my act together enough. Bess says that's hogwash of the highest order – that there is never a good time to have children and that whatever you do to get yourself organized, it's a lost cause. There are just some things in life you can't totally prepare yourself for. You are forced to do a lot of learning on the job in real time, like global teamwork really.

GO MEET THE ENIGMAS

'WILL!'

'Coming SHE.'

'Nice work so far on the briefing report,' she said, offering me an extra Caffeine Tornado she had picked up on the way in. 'I must owe you at least one of these,' she said smirking.

'I think eleven would be more accurate,' I answered, 'but only an utterly pathetic soul would keep a record and store it on his or her smart phone.' I pulled out my phone and placed it on her desk with a wink and a smile.

'Glad you're here to keep me honest and organized Will. Have you spoken to the Enigmas yet?'

'Who?'

'Tomas and Theresa at Boffin Labs in Bloomsbury, near the British Museum. They were the principal designers of our good friend GO*dz*W*illa.*'

'Oh I see. No, I haven't. First I've heard of them.'

'Sorry Will. I should have mentioned them. Slipped through my sagging neural network. But wait, do you mean to say you've been here over a month and aren't able to read my mind yet? Shame on you!'

'Put it down to stolen caffeine opportunities,' I retorted.

For the first time, I noticed that SHE had a picture of a woman, a bit younger than herself, on her windowsill. The woman had the same look of summer and champagne that SHE had, although there was a touch more melancholy about her. This must be SHE's PARTNER! I could definitely see them as a couple.

After a short deliberation with myself, I decided not to ask any questions. It's a funny thing, but if it had been a man's picture, I would have felt OK about enquiring – husband, boyfriend? Knowing that SHE is gay made me shy of asking, but if she has put a picture of this woman on her windowsill, does that signal her openness to questions? Is SHE's 'gayness' now in the shared public realm? Is it rude to ask or not to ask? It's so confusing. There's also the fact that the picture is on the windowsill and not close by her on the desk. Does that mean she wants to keep the picture somewhat out of the public gaze? Help me someone. I'm not waving, but drowning.

I called Boffin Labs. Dates were difficult to coordinate, but I arranged to meet Tomas and Theresa for a brief afternoon tea next Thursday at the Court Restaurant in the British Museum.

GO*dz*Wi*lla*: OUR GLOBAL OFFICE WORKSPACE

I haven't told you much yet about *The Fun House's* own virtual Global Office Workspace called GO*dz*W*illa*. The system was launched last year, and the idea is to provide us all with a shared work space and a degree of unified communications for generating and sharing knowledge.

When I log on each morning, my avatar (created from a picture snapped of me daily by my computer) appears in the onscreen entrance to the GO*dz*W*illa* offices. This virtual office space is where we all spend most of our time when we're at work, and so is as real to us as the physical office spaces we sit in.

Imagine on your screen a visual of a steel, brick, wood, and glass office space (very clean looking and postmodern, which is actually very different from the old warehouse space we rent on the South Bank of the Thames). In the foreground of the screen is the main lobby area that you can custom-design yourself. For example, in mine (bottom left of screen) I have a glass table on which sits a computer. This gives me immediate access to the basic applications I use and to the Internet. On the same table sits a world clock, a dictionary and thesaurus, a cultural awareness and information database, language translator, and a calculator. They all expand into active windows when I click on them. In the middle of my lobby is a TV screen on which I get RSS feeds. At the bottom right-hand corner of the screen is *The Wit's End Café*. If you feel in need of a spark of creativity or even a mental diversion, clicking there will display surreal images and random words on your screen to get the brain circuits sparking. If anyone else is in the *Café*, you can, of course, just chat to each other.

On the far left side of the virtual office is the entrance, and, as I've mentioned already, that's where your avatar first appears after logging on.

Enough about GO*dz*W*illa* for now. I'm overdosing on e-mails, phone calls, and instant messages. I'm a pretty good multitasker, but even I have my limits. I need to set some rules for myself, e.g. don't respond to e-mails immediately after they come in. Maybe just check my inbox when I come into work, twice in the morning, immediately after lunch, and twice in the afternoon. I could also, I suppose, only turn on instant messaging at certain times, although I do notice panicky withdrawal symptoms if I feel I'm not connected. I could turn off my cell phone, but that might be falling too deep into the Bottomless Pit of Nonexistence.

SUDDEN INTEREST IN FAMILY VALUES

Spinks came into the *House* today with a framed photo of two young, fresh-faced, and freckled children climbing on a garden gate. I asked him who they were. 'My ... nephew and niece,' he said hesitatingly.

'Good looking kids. Your brother's or sister's?' I asked.

'Brother's,' he said urgently. 'Brother, Winston. My sister Margaret isn't married yet.'

'Did you take the picture? Looks very professional.'

'Um ... no. Margaret took it with her new digital.'

'Excellent. She's talented.'

'Yes. Always was the brightest of the bunch.'

'Why the sudden interest in putting the family on display?' I asked. It was intrusive I know, but Spinks had never had any photos or personal things on or around his desk before.

'Important to uphold family in these turbulent times. Families are the stabilising force in a world gone mad, don't you know? Now, more than ever, Britain needs the rock solid foundation of its families.' I wasn't sure if my own wacky family deserved such accolades, but .... He picked up his phone and called Maintenance; his chair was not rotating. I hadn't touched it, I swear.

WEBS ARE IT!

Sophie sent me a web link today that took me to a site displaying spider webs. These weren't ordinary webs, but those created by spiders fed on drug-dosed flies. It was interesting to see the variations from *normal* in webs influenced by LSD, mescaline, and hashish. Sophie was highlighting the fact that the web created by the caffeine-intoxicated spider was barely a web at all, just a few haphazard threads. Don't get me wrong. Sophie is not advocating that I drop caffeine and start experimenting with illegal substances. She's just worried that my intake of Caffeine Tornados needs to be dramatically controlled before I lose any ability to coordinate myself. She says that when we hug, she can feel my whole body buzzing. I think that's actually more to do with her than caffeine!

What Sophie's e-mail really made me think about was overstimulation. How we might damage our virtual webs by too much *digicaffeine*. Too much information demanding too much attention in too many places too much of the time.

INVITE TO PURGATORY

My brother-in-law Noel called this morning to invite me for the weekend. Noel is a shy, introverted soul and I know my sister forces him to get on the phone and make these social arrangement calls. Noel and my sister live in Brighton on the south coast, and he teaches philosophy at the local university. Noel finds it difficult to engage in small talk, so it wasn't too much of a surprise when he suddenly – completely out of the blue – asked why I thought it took him so long to wash his hair; he doesn't have much left except for a long red combover that stands up like a lopsided parrot's crest in the slightest wind. Having been thinking a lot about coordination and organization, I said, 'Because you have to find it first.' It was cruel I know and I think he took it badly. He said he would put my sister Bess on the phone.

I thanked Bess for the invite and told her I would be bringing along the new love of my life, Sophie. I had only managed to get out a few words about her when Bess said, 'She's too good for you.' Isn't family supposed to be supportive? Isn't unconditional love and nurturing supposed to be part of the package? *Note to self: be sure to buy Em and Seb something that will drive Bess and Noel crazy. Something electronic, noisy, and hypersteroidal. Woooohoooooo.*

INTO THE GUTS OF GOdzWilla

Earlier, I described the lobby of our virtual workspace. Now let me take you deeper inside the beast.

The back wall of the office is divided into upper and lower floors. On each floor are doors leading into different rooms. The left-hand door on the lower back wall is the Hello/Goodbye (HG) Room. By clicking on the door of that room, you will enter into an open plan office space in which you will see the avatars of those currently online. In the HG room you can warp your avatar photo so that it expresses different emotions; you can change it during the day if your mood changes.[9] If the room is crowded, you can click on your team name in an options box and see only your team members who are online. If you click on an avatar, it will tell you if that person is available, how that person would

---

[9] A system called Face Alive Icons – developed by Xin Li, University of Pittsburgh – allows you to take an image of your own face and to warp your facial features to communicate different moods. See 'The New Face of Emotions' by Duncan Graham-Rowe in *Technology Review*, 27 March 2007.

like to be communicated with at this time, as well as the hours they prefer to be reached – if not now. You can also access a personal profile, as well as that person's current thoughts on what projects they are working on, or even their thoughts about life in general. This is to help make what we are doing and thinking as explicit as possible. We call this feature the Clog, which is short for Consciousness Log. I suppose it's really a mini Blog or Bloggette. Input is made either via typing or voice recognition software, and you can update your Clog at any time, even from your phone. I check in with some Clogs first thing in the morning to catch up on personal news and ideas. My favourite update was from Moonbeam: 'Last night I did some reading on Complexity Theory. Fantastic! I've decided to mix up all the paper files in the London office. We'll work at the edge of chaos from now on, and this will increase the emergence of new thinking.'

Nobody thought Moonbeam would actually do such a thing, but she did! She came in one weekend and woooosh, the filing system was suddenly based on the juxtaposition of opposites (no, that suggests more order than there actually is). Nothing has emerged from the new system yet except loud kicking and banging of drawers, and more than colour-ful cursing – mostly from Moonbeam herself who seems to have some regrets about conjuring up the edge of chaos genie.

IN THE FAMILY WAY

I bumped into Moonbeam in *Has Bean* this morning. She couldn't stop laughing – and was almost in tears – as she told me about her latest discovery. The night before, she had been out shopping for a birthday present for her mother. What does she find in one shop, but the same frame and photo that Spinks now has on his desk!

'No, I don't believe it,' I snorted, causing some alarm among the *Has Bean* staff. 'What an absolutely world-class phony.'

'I thought I'd wet myself when I saw it,' Moonbeam went on. 'Anyway, I bought one to put on the table in our little conference area. Thought it would cheer the place up a bit.'

'I can't believe he did that. What possessed him?'

'I was talking with one of my friends, and she says quite a few men are doing it these days; something to do with research done in America.[10] Women, it seems, choose child-friendly men for long-term relationships. According to my friend, women can tell when a man is or is not fond of children by looking at their face.'

'So the photo is all in aid of helping Spinks get a date?'

'I suppose. He doesn't have a very child-adoring face, so the picture might help.'

DEEPER INTO THE BELLY OF THE BEAST

I noticed this morning that the Spinks family photo had disappeared from his desk. He must have come across the one Moonbeam put in the conference room. Ha ha! Would have loved to have filmed his reaction. A priceless YouTube moment!

In the last entry I made about GO*dz*W*illa*, I had taken you into the HG Room. Next door is the Calendar Room. This is where the central diary is kept for everyone in *The Fun House*. When you enter someone's diary, you can click on a specific date and leave a voice message asking for a suitable meeting time; or you can type in your request. You can also keep logs in there for tracking use of time; this makes it relatively easy to see how much a particular project is costing us.

Alongside the Calendar Room is the Blueprint Room. After the initial creative thinking has been done, a project starts with a detailed plan and budget. These need to be

---

[10] Research from a team at the University of California, Santa Barbara, and reported in an article called 'Oochy woochy coochy coo' in *The Economist*, 13 May 2006.

updated regularly by project leaders. Within the plans, you can also see what tasks are dependent on one another, and identify critical paths. This makes project management relatively simple, although it also sends the more creative types into rages against the Corporate GO*dz*W*illa* Machine.

Next to the Blueprint Room is the Data Room. Inside is the current information related to active projects, e.g. e-mails, designs, project status reports, and prototype test results. Information related to nonactive projects is stored in the Library, which is the last room on the right-hand side of the lower floor. In the Library, I can also access e-learning modules on useful skills.

I'm making all of these rooms sound like they are totally separate from one another, but that's not the case. There are all sorts of features enabling you to bring items from different rooms together. For example, the contents of the Blueprint and Data rooms can be brought together and stored in what we call a 'Hot Tub'. This can also hold final versions of relevant wiki documents, and presentations and notes from web meetings. Hot Tubs can be accessed by all project team members, even those from outside *The Fun House* firewall.

OK, WEBS *AND* COLONIES ARE IT!

It's not that I'm a particularly reflective person – too much to *do* to spend time gazing at the belly button – but as I was making my way home on the Underground last night, I listened to a podcast about how smart ants are. Did you know that when ants are intoxicated, they always fall over on their right side? That, of course, raises the question: If ants are so smart why do they get intoxicated? Ha ha, I can talk!

An ant colony, it appears, is a *superorganism*, which means that the colony itself seems to operate as a single being, while consisting of millions of individual beings. So, the question is, how does the complex behaviour of the whole colony arise from the interactions of its many parts?

What do the individuals do to create and sustain the whole? Sounds like it could be useful to global virtual teams.[11]

According to the podcast, there are only two ways to achieve the high levels of coordination found in the ant colony: top-down hierarchical control or the bottom-up approach in which individuals follow a small number of rules. Even though ant colonies have queens, it seems they are not positioned at the top of a controlling hierarchy. The order arises from the behaviour of individual workers.

When needing a new source of food, ants explore randomly. When the food is found, the ants return back to the colony while leaving a pheromone trail (a pheromone is a chemical(s) transmitting messages to members of the same species). Other ants will follow this trail, reinforcing it as they do so. When the food supply is diminished, fewer ants are attracted and so the trail is reinforced less and less. I suppose one of the rules for the ants is to follow the trail with the stronger smell. Apparently there is a whole field of study called ant colony optimization (ACO) that develops probabilistic tools for use in network routing, transportation systems, and data mining.

What's the bottom line for virtual teams? I think it's in developing a set of operating rules that guide individual behaviours in support of the whole. I should have thought about that more, but after the podcast my head was hurting. I switched my iPod to *The Smashing Pumpkins* and let them take me to another place.

GOING UP

On the upper level of GO*dz*W*illa* are several other rooms. The first two rooms on the left-hand side are for Communications. Communication Room 'A' is for asynchronous

---

[11] If you are interested in nature's lessons for virtual teams, see Ken Thompson's newsletter at www.bioteaming.com.

communication methods.[12] From there you can send e-mails, set up a threaded discussion, or create a wiki[13] page for review and editing. We're using wikis more and more because it cuts down on e-mail traffic and the multiple versions of documents that some poor soul used to collate and try to make sense of. The next door to the right is Communication Room 'S'. In there you can use synchronous communication[14] methods like Instant Messaging, VoIP (for individual and conference calls), and web conferencing with or without video (we all have web cams if we want to use them). If we need to use a more sophisticated video technology we can go to a Telepresence[15] facility. One great feature about GO*dz*W*illa* is that you can launch a web conference with a click of the mouse; this is great for having spontaneous meetings. There's no downloading of software from the web when you want a meeting and no frustrating wait times while you try to disable firewalls, allow popups, or download Java. Our web meeting technology allows us to replicate a live meeting through video, audio, use of whiteboards, and sharing of applications such as spreadsheets.

We don't do a lot of the large-scale webinars[16] anymore; we have the capability, but the smaller joint work meetings are how we do most of our work. One 'big brother' feature in our webinars is the attention monitoring system.[17] If I'm giving a webinar, I can see who in the audience is really

---

[12] Asynchronous – communication taking place at different times, e.g. e-mail.

[13] Wiki – web software enabling collaborative writing and editing. Go to www.wikispot.org and create your own.

[14] Synchronous – communication taking place in real-time, e.g. Instant Messaging.

[15] Telepresence – technological step-up from videoconferencing that aims at producing a feeling of 'being there'.

[16] A web conference/seminar in which most of the communication is one-way from presenter to audience.

[17] Software from Citrix Online – GoToWebinar – has a dashboard through which the webinar organizer can monitor the attentiveness of attendees.

paying attention. If someone in my webinar is also doing their e-mail or searching the web, their attention score will go down on my screen! If sales people are doing a webinar for customers, this allows them to target their follow-up calls to those paying the most attention. If the sales person sends out the presentation after the webinar, he or she can also track if the presentation is seen again, who sees it, and how it gets forwarded. Yes, this is the world of viral presentations[18] folks!

Next is the Imagine Room. This is set up for electronic brainstorming and innovation. Project members can enter the room with partners, suppliers, retail customers and end-users to work on game ideas, process improvements, new system needs, and so on.

One door further to the right is the Games Room. Part of this room is used to communicate a concept to the gaming community. It is a public, open source site in which users can apply their own imaginations and improve the concept. Another part of this room is used for testers to 'play' with prototype games. Testers give direct feedback to the project team on design, navigation, bugs, and perceived entertainment value.

In the London Office we have one tester – Webster 'The Bugster' Rushkoff. The Bugster is a mystery to everyone. He's here when people arrive in the morning and when they leave at night. He only speaks when spoken to, and even then his responses are pretty inaudible. He sits in a corner of the office with his blonde dreadlocks covering much of his face, his ever-smelly brown tee-shirt hanging on his don't-even-think-of-offering-me-red-meat-body, faded denim jeans that could stand to attention unaided, and combat boots. His eyes are forever locked on to the screen world of crashes, explosions, madness, and mayhem.

---

[18] Brainshark (www.brainshark.com) has developed software to track the viral spread of presentations.

The very last room is the Workout Room. If you're tired or stressed, you can enter the room, click on 'Energize Me' and you'll be shown a random set of physical exercises you can do at or near your desk with your avatar.

GO*dz*W*illa* was developed *with* game players, and so there are occasional surprises for the user. Last week, I accidentally hit two keys when typing 'Fun House'. Up pops an evil-looking baby Godzilla that kicks my misspelled word right off the document and into the wastebasket icon! These features can get annoying, so the designers kindly allow us to turn them off.

Another game feature is the use of support agents or bots.[19] These are 'intelligent' software tools of varying degrees of sophistication that you can chat with (the speech is unscripted); you can even ask their advice about using a particular technology, ask for hints, send them on an errand (e.g. search the database for ...), and complete a task (calculate ... or contact ...).

FINDING THE SWEET SPOT

On my way to meet with the Enigmas, I called into a toyshop on Regent Street. There, sitting on a shelf between a robotic puppy and a Dr Who Dalek, was the perfect gift for the Purgatories – an electronic, roaring, and sparking Godzilla complete with a tall building that would collapse when punched by the rampaging monster. Most excellent!

When I found Tomas and Theresa, I was quite taken aback. Theresa was the woman in the picture on SHE's windowsill! So, this is SHE's PARTNER! Yes, I can see even clearer that they belong together. They both have a smart but unpretentious air about them.

---

[19] Bot is short for 'robot'. These software tools are most commonly used for data mining. Go to www.blogspot.com where you can download some for free!

It was exciting in a way. I felt I had suddenly become initiated into a club whose members were the guardians of secret knowledge. Tomas was a large, somewhat dapper character with swept-back greying hair gathered into a short ponytail and a Van Dyke beard. He wore a loose black silk suit, pink and blue striped buttoned down shirt, and a red silk scarf knotted at the neck and flowing down to his waist. Over his shoulders was draped a classic Burberry trench coat.

I hadn't really done any thinking about the kind of conversation the three of us would have, and at first it meandered. Tomas loved to talk – or at least lecture – but unfortunately his academic descriptions of symbiotic organizational forms and task synchronization mechanisms made my eyes glaze over. Theresa could see my distress and thankfully began to lead the conversation. 'I think we should start at the beginning,' she said, 'and lead you through the thinking and design process as it unfolded. We'll probably make it sound much neater than it was, but you should be able to see the reasoning that went into GO*dz*W*illa*.' I agreed wholeheartedly, while Tomas seemed to anticipate that such a pedestrian approach could only lead to frightful boredom on his part. He focused his attention on the scones and sandwiches that had arrived at the table, and started flirting with one of the waitresses.

'OK. To begin with,' said Theresa, 'we had to ask some very basic questions. You know, the what, why, who, where, and how questions. Let's start with the "what" question.'

'In designing a coordination space like GO*dz*W*illa*, it's best to keep the primary objective in sight at all times. In the case of *The Fun House* we were to concentrate the distributed feelings, thoughts, and actions of global team members on achieving the design, development, and delivery of highly engaging electronic games. So, some keywords relevant to thinking about this space included: synchronization, coherence, and continuity. You want the space contributing to helping colleagues separated by distances and cultures to manage the many uncertainties they face.'

'You make the space sound like an active participant in the teamwork,' I said.

'That's exactly the point. It's the way architects talk about space; in our case, it's virtual space.' I was reminded of Sunil's earlier reference to virtual architecture.

'That's good. I like that. But don't people want to use the space in different ways?' I argued.

'Good point,' said Theresa, which boosted my ego, but made Tomas roll his eyes. 'We knew that in creating GO*dz*Willa we were trying to create an optimum blend of opposites. On the one side you have the need for control and predictability and on the other is the need for creativity and unpredictability. What we tried to do in GO*dz*Willa was to create a middle path, a shared space in which both could coexist. We needed to help users find the coordination sweet spot for themselves.'

'Sweet spot?'

'Yes. It's often used to describe the point on a racquet or a bat where you get the most *zing* when you hit the ball.'

'Yes, OK.'

'I think it's also used in body piercing,' added Tomas through a mouthful of scone, strawberry jam, and clotted cream. 'If you were to have your nose pierced, for example, the sweet spot would be somewhere between the nasal cartilage and the bottom of your nose. Ask Moonbeam, I'm sure she'll be able to tell you.'

'You know Moonbeam?' I asked.

'Oh yes. Moonbeam is actually a sweet spot in her own right,' he said grinning.

'Let's get back to GO*dz*Willa,' said Theresa, showing some impatience with Tomas. 'There won't be just one sweet spot in a coordination space because different people with different roles and functions are doing different work.

'As you know, there are lots of different types of work needing to be done in the space, and some require more coordination than others. Some tasks are just one-off; they'll rarely be repeated, if ever. Others are repeated over and over. We also know that individuals working alone will perform some tasks, while others need input from a wider group. Some tasks have high value and others moderate or low value. Some need to be done in the short or medium term, and others in the longer term. A number of tasks will need to be done in sequence while others can be in parallel. People will contribute to the common goal in different ways, and rather than forcing people to conform absolutely to the space *we* wanted to create, we wanted them to make the space their own as much as possible.'

'Couldn't that be chaotic?' I said, thinking of Moonbeam's hurtling-over-the-edge-of-chaos filing disaster.

'Yes, but it was a question of thinking through where we needed to provide some order, predictability, and control – as in budgetary processes, for example – and where there could be freer, open-ended space as in early creative design. It's all about the space being directional *and* adaptive. I suppose it approaches what some would call a "chaordic" environment.' *Note to self: tell Moonbeam to do some reading on this asap.*

Tomas had finished with his share of scones and sandwiches – as well of some of Theresa's and mine – and wandered off to find the toilets. 'Tomas is a man with big appetites,' said Theresa.

Not being particularly interested in Tomas' appetites, I stayed focused on coordination. 'I suppose,' I went on, 'that how the coordination space gets used will also depend on the different types of teams making use of it.'

'That's true. I think about team needs and appropriate coordination spaces as a trio (I feel an acronym coming on, I thought, and I was right). Think in terms of tIPE. Teams (t) at different times require spaces that enable innovation (I), planning (P), and execution (E). Teams focused on innovation – or who are in an innovation phase – need an open coordination and collaboration space in which they can brainstorm, research, play, and communicate widely. Tasks needing this kind of space tend to be nonroutine and the outcomes uncertain.

'Teams focused on planning need a space that supports them in defining and consolidating who they are. The requirement here is for a more structured space with room for a team charter and project planning tools.

'A team with a focus on execution is aimed at producing specific outcomes in terms of designs, specifications, code, product prototypes, marketing plans, and so on. These teams need a synchronization space; if they are not closely aligned they are wasteful of time and other resources. They really need tools like online calendars, role and responsibility matrices, project maps, project logs, progress dashboards, decision parameter guidelines, communication planning tools, and so on. It needs to be a transparent space in which everyone can see clearly what is going on within the team so that potential problems can be spotted quickly and dealt with proactively.'

'You know what I really like in GO*dz*W*illa*,' I said, 'are the templates, maps and other tools you provide. You even have those Avatar Pilots offering advice on how to run an effective web meeting or a teleconference, etcetera.'

'Yes, all of the common tools and templates help provide some sense of continuity and coherence.'

'How did you arrive at those because there must be differences in how people around the world want to do things?'

'Yes, but you often find there is more agreement than you might think. We held virtual focus groups with *Fun House* people from around the world to talk about how they would like to see GO*dz*W*illa* work. Most agreed on the common tools. There were some style differences in communication that we had to work out.'

'For example?'

'It's pretty common knowledge that many people in Asia aren't comfortable with the brainstorming style. They feel there is too much danger of losing face. So, we built in asynchronous and synchronous communication functions that allow people to contribute anonymously. Feedback we've had from Asia is very positive about that.'

Over Theresa's shoulder I could see Tomas talking somewhat heatedly with the waitress he had been flirting with at our table. At one point he took her by the arm and seemed to shake her, but she wrenched herself away and walked off towards the kitchen. This was obviously not their first meeting. Interesting!

'In reality, of course,' Theresa went on, 'most teams need to mix the different types of space. Coordination needs can be quite fluid.'

Looking over Theresa's shoulder again, I saw that the waitress had exited from the kitchen and Tomas was once more haranguing her. At one point she put down her tray of tea, scones, and sandwiches and slapped his face. Even more interesting!

Tomas returned to the table looking a little flushed and angry. Theresa asked if he was OK to which he answered, 'Bit of an upset stomach.' He ordered more scones and sandwiches from another waitress, although Theresa said that might not be wise if he wasn't feeling well.

The conversation never really picked up again after Tomas came back. I could see his eyes hurling daggers at the young woman who had waited on us earlier and hers hurling spears back at him. Tomas finished off his third pot of tea, and then the three of us exchanged goodbyes. Theresa gave me a hug when we parted and said, 'Give Sheila a hug from me, Will.' I thought that a bit strange, given that in an hour or so they would probably be sitting on a couch together, sipping some red wine, and talking about their days at the office. Maybe they were partners, but didn't actually live together. Is it any of my business? No? Am I curious? Of course!

Tomas took my right hand in both of his, said 'Adieu, my friend,' adjusted his Burberry trench coat, donned a Mink Russian Trooper hat, and swept dramatically towards the stairs. Theresa said she had thought of a few more things to tell me and would call in the next few days.

OOPS

'So Will, I hear you met my sister and brother-in-law,' said SHE. 'I hope Tomas was on his best behaviour.'

'Your sister and brother-in-law … right. Yes, indeed.' I felt like a complete idiot for not having made the connection between SHE and Theresa. My mind was so focused on SHE being gay that it had made up its own story about the two of them.

'I'm not sure how Theresa puts up with Tomas and his Casanova complex,' she went on. 'Brilliant mind, but the morals of a goat. He tried to hit on me at their wedding! I hear from Theresa that he's having a fling with a waitress at the British Museum. My darling sister could do so much better.'

PLAYING BY THE RULES

Theresa called me this afternoon. Her warm, sunny voice gave no hint of any trouble behind the scenes. 'I just wanted to finish the conversation we were having the other day Will. Is now a good time?'

'Yes, absolutely. Thanks for phoning.'

'Remember the other evening when I talked about different coordination spaces needed for different focus activities on teams?'

'Yes.'

'If high-level coordination is to exist on a team then shared rules for individuals are also a must.'

'Like an ant colony,' I said, feeling pleased with yours truly.

'My Will, so you're not just a pretty face.' To say that I blushed beet red is a gross understatement. Moonbeam actually walked over to see if I was OK.

'I do,' I said, which Moonbeam took to mean I was accepting a proposal. She rushed off to tell everyone I had just become engaged. Restrained applause and cheering broke out which made the blushing even worse.

'Let me send you the 10 behavioural rules we defined for *The Fun House*. I'll e-mail them to you right now.'

'OK. But how come I don't already know them?'

'Hmm, I'm not the one to ask about that. … Did you get them?'

'Hang on. Yes, looking at them now.'

- Be Accessible – keep the communication channels as open as possible.
- Be Alert – always be on the lookout for emerging trends, opportunities, and threats.
- Be Aligned – act consistently with others in following the rules.
- Be Connected – reach out to others with similar interests and issues.
- Be Informative – always share what you know.
- Be Innovative – identify problems, solve them, learn, and keep going.
- Be Present – show others you are there with them as much as possible.
- Be Responsible – take personal ownership and take action.
- Be Thoughtful – show consideration for others on the team.
- Be Transparent – keep your thinking and actions visible to everyone.

'I can see how various features of GO*dz*W*illa* fit with these rules. I think the Clogs and the threaded discussions help team members to be alert and transparent. The Hello/ Goodbye Room also helps maintain a sense of presence.'

'Right. As I said the other day, the coordination space is itself a player in the game of work.'

'Many thanks for this Theresa. It will be very useful. Give my best to Tomas.'

'Ah yes, the elusive and inscrutable Tomas. Bye Will.' I could hear the dark wind of depression rattle her voice as she signed off and I felt bad for her.

When I had finished the call, several people rushed over to offer congratulations on my engagement. Nisha said she must throw a party. They all deflated quickly when I said there would be no such party on my account.

Before leaving that night, I asked Moonbeam if she knew about the sweet spot in her nasal septum.

'You've been talking with that animal Tomas,' she snapped at me. 'Just keep him away from me, Will.'

LOSING IT

When Spinks came back from lunch today, he spat 'You disgust me,' as he passed by my desk. He then waddled off in the direction of the toilets. He seems to be doing that a lot lately – maybe premature prostate problems.

I looked around at others in the office to see if I could gather any clues about what was on Spinks' tiny mind. Faces averted themselves from mine and became intently focused on the computer monitor closest to them. I walked over to Moonbeam who held up her hand signalling that she didn't want to speak.

'What?' I said. 'What was that all about?' Moonbeam shook her head while forcing out an almost inaudible 'No, no' from tightly pursed lips. 'Please,' I asked again, 'what is it?' Moonbeam looked up at me tearfully, and said, 'You should really talk to Sadie.'

'Sadie? Why Sadie? Oh God ... no ... what's happened to her?' I tore out of the room and up the stairs to the next level where Sadie's office was located.

She was sitting at her computer surrounded by some of the marketing people. They saw me coming and cleared a path. Sadie had obviously been crying, but she hastily wiped the tears from her cheeks when she saw me. She took a deep breath and stared at her monitor not wanting to make eye contact with me.

'Let it go, Will,' she said in a breathy whisper.

'Let what go Sadie?'

'I don't want to talk about it. Just let it go.'

'How can I let go of something I don't have a hold of?'

Someone tugged at my arm. I turned to see Julian Cuthbert, one of the retail marketing specialists. He quietly asked me to go out into the hallway with him.

'It was Spinks,' he said. 'He was sitting close by Sadie and some of her friends at lunch. They were talking about the time that you and Sadie used to be a couple, and Spinks obviously overheard.'

'So what? I don't understand.'

'He suddenly stood up and screamed at her, saying things like, "Why the hell don't you stick to your black brothers?"'

All I remember is a wild … howling … rage surge through me as I crashed back down the stairs.

Spinks saw me tearing towards him and bolted back into the toilets. As I crashed through the door, he was locking himself inside a cubicle.

'Leave me alone,' he screeched. 'I'll call the police … oh God don't hurt me.'

He shrieked hysterically as I leapt on to the toilet seat in the next cubicle and yanked myself up on to the top of the wall separating us. I could hear other screaming and shouting in the toilet as I punched the walls and hurled every obscenity known to man (and woman) at Spinks. He had hunched himself into a tight fetal position on the floor out of my reach. My right foot was able to gain leverage on the back wall and I started to slide over on to his side. 'God might not hurt you, but I will, you (censored, censored, censored).'

Suddenly there seemed to be many hands tugging at my legs. I was kicking at the air trying to gain more leverage to take me over the wall when I felt my left foot connect with someone. Eventually the hands of Sadie, Nisha, Moonbeam, Julian and SHE pulled me back down.

I saw Nisha was trying to stem blood from her nose and my rage flipped in an instant to absolutely misery. 'Oh Nisha, no. I'm so, so sorry,' I said pitifully. 'Let me get some ice.'

SHE grabbed me by the shoulders. 'Go home Will. Go home now. We'll take care of Nisha. Go home and take care of your hands.' Looking down, I could see that I might have broken some fingers on my right hand. 'Work at home for the rest of the week,' SHE went on. 'Call me tomorrow and we'll talk about this.'

The hurt I had done to Nisha, and SHE's pleading voice, drained me of any rage I had left. I walked out of the office into the wind and the rain, and the cold slapped my face. I had left my jacket, but I wasn't going to go back inside to get it – no way. Every part of me seemed to radiate pain and not even the bitter chill could anaesthetize me. Blindly and miserably, I walked the long soaking miles back to my flat.

I told Sophie the whole story. She sympathized, but was surprised at my extreme reaction. Quietly, she asked me if I still had feelings for Sadie. I told her no, but I don't think she believed me. I'm not sure I believe it myself.

Later, I called Bess. 'You know you've always said I avoid conflict. Well today it found me and I didn't handle its visit very well; in fact, I have three broken fingers to prove that I didn't. There is also Nisha's bloody nose as evidence against me. I won't be making it down to see you this weekend, Sis.'

'Then I'll be coming up to see you, Will.'

CAPABILITY

AFTERMATH

There wasn't really enough room for me to work in my one-room-and-a-saucepan-flat so I stayed with Sophie. Her skepticism about my feelings for Sadie remained. I told her the racist bullying had made me snap, and of course it had. But if the person being bullied had been someone other than Sadie, would I have reacted so violently?

I called SHE and we talked the incident through. She was very understanding, but of course she can't have vigilantes tearing around the toilets trying to right wrongs. I can go back next week, and as I can still access GO*dz*W*illa* from Sophie's place, there will actually be very little interruption.

'I never expected to find myself thrust into an episode of *24*,'[20] SHE said. 'I was quite surprised that I was able to stay relatively calm and not tear Spinks apart myself.'

'What's happened to him?' I asked, with bitterness still evident in my voice.

'He's still here, but I've put him on three month's probation. If he demonstrates any further racist behaviour, he'll be out faster than *you* can throw a punch at a wall. I've also had him apologize publicly to Sadie. If he didn't, he was

---

[20] A TV show broadcast by Fox in the US – and syndicated around the world – that stars Kiefer Sutherland as Los Angeles Counter Terrorism Unit agent Jack Bauer. Violence in the service of the greater good is a common theme in each series.

going to have to leave right then and damn the consequences. I've also moved him downstairs to keep him more
out of your way.'

'Downstairs he'll be next to Maintenance. He already
gives them a lot of grief.'

'I'm sure they will handle Mr Spinks in their own way.'

This was going to be interesting because most of the
people in Maintenance were either immigrants from Central
and Eastern Europe or sons of the sons of immigrants from
the West Indies.

I also spoke to Sadie over the phone. She said it was all
very heroic, but really, really stupid! I could have lost my
job, been charged with assault, and hurt myself worse than
I had. But she loved me still … as a friend.

One evening I visited Nisha and her family, and I apologized as profusely as I could. They were very kind and
generous, even feeding me a fabulous lamb curry and home-
made nan bread. Luckily Nisha's nose hadn't been broken,
just bloodied and bruised. Her youngest son, Vikram, asked
me if I was the man who had beaten up his mother?

During the meal, Nisha talked about bigotry. 'When you
are confronting it you are not dealing with reason or logic,
but emotion.' She feels that while I have been away she has
actually made some progress with the insecure Spinks. He
had told her that he had let his feelings get the better of him
and that perhaps he had gone too far, which was something,
I suppose. He even drank a cup of her Earl Grey tea and
thought it was excellent. He was surprised by her kindness
because he felt everyone would treat him like an outcast.
He is an outcast as far as I'm concerned. I'm not sure I'm
capable of Nisha's generosity of spirit.

THE GREAT ESCAPE

First day back on my commute. This morning I rode the
Underground listening to REM's *Daysleeper,* which seems to
have become my anthem with all my late night and early

morning conference calls. Beside me a tall, immaculately dressed, eagle-nosed gent was hovering over his newspaper mumbling something about the rotten state of Britain and all these foreigners. His superior nose was stuck so high in the air it was in danger of becoming a pigeon perch. AND THEN, without any warning the train suddenly SLAMMED to a halt and ... WHOOSH... . off came his toupee straight into the lap of a young woman who had been quietly minding her own business. Her shrill cries of disgust and horror filled the carriage as we rolled into the next station. We all tried not to look at her, but of course we couldn't help ourselves. There she sat shaking and crying with what looked like a dead rat in her lap. The owner stood paralysed to the spot, the nose much less aloft. We all wondered what the victim would do next. Would she leap up and let the chestnut tuft fall on the feet of those standing close by? Who knows what stir that would have created? Would she be brave enough to pick it up in her trembling fingers and give it back to the scarlet-faced owner? Or would she jump from the train as soon as the doors opened?

Actually, what happened was that a kindly neighbour picked it up from her lap with the tip of a smart-looking fountain pen, wrapped it up in his newspaper, and had the now desperately-trying-not-to-wet-themselves-with-laughter crowd pass it back over their heads to the mortified owner. He grabbed the offending fur, stuffed it into a trouser pocket, and tried to get through the crowd to the doors. Unfortunately, he didn't make it in time to exit. For his agonising ride to the next station, he stood with his nose pressed hard against the doors hoping that somehow they would open and the dark tunnel would swallow him up. When we did eventually arrive at the next station, he bolted towards the escalator like someone who knows his five-day bout of constipation is about to come to an abrupt, rip-roaring end.

I love to watch the pompous come crashing down from their self-made pedestals. Don't you? Woooooooohooooooo. However, it was another missed YouTube opportunity.

Is there a lesson in here? Yes. If you're going to do something, like wear a toupee, take on a new job, learn a new piece of software, or work virtually across the globe, do it right. Learn what it takes to keep your self-esteem intact and avoid embarrassing, or creating a nuisance for, others.

A LOST GENERATION? (OR IS IT JUST MY PARENTS?)

'Darling!'

Despite the noise on the line, and without another word being spoken, I knew it was my mother – Beverly, the Mae West of the Midlands the Scarily Self-Absorbed Diva of Amateur Theatricals.

'Have you heard from your father lately dear? Last I heard from him was a postcard from the town of Shrewsbury a couple of weeks ago. He was playing around in some old Roman ruins nearby. Can't remember the name – sounded a bit like those warts you get on the bottom of your feet.'

'Verrucas?'

'Something like that.'

'I think you mean Viriconium,' I said, 'also known as Wroxeter.'

'Well, I need him to help with the Christmas show,' continued my mother. 'He's so inconsiderate. I wish he'd learn to use that mobile phone you bought him.'

I knew that was an unlikely proposition. Two years before the phone, I'd bought him a VCR player and given him my ancient collection of videos. After a power cut, the time display had returned to flashing zeros and needed to be reset. Did he fix the time? No. Next time I went home there was a piece of masking tape over where the time display should have been.

A conversation with my mother isn't really a conversation at all. She's either saying to me 'Why can't you be more like _____' (fill in a name, any name will do) or she complains bitterly about how uncooperative the world is. My father is usually the target of her barbs.

'If you hear from him Darling, would you tell him his wife needs him immediately!'

'Yes, of course.'

I don't like to go out in public with my mother. It is 'darling' this and 'darling' that. She's morphed herself into a theatrical stereotype and can't escape.

When I put the phone down, I tried to imagine my parents working somewhere like *The Fun House* where using technology is as natural as breathing. I was thinking of buying my father a digital camera for Christmas, but I'd just be deluding myself that he'll ever be able to use it to photograph his beloved Roman ruins – and why would I want to add to the self-delusion in the world?

THE CONVERSATION BEGINS

I've told you before that in GO*dz*W*illa* we have an asynchronous communications room. One feature of the room is that we can set up a conversation area (Forum) in which we can have threaded discussions. These are asynchronous text-based group discussions within a folder where someone posts a message. Others can reply in their own time to the message that has been posted, and these responses are linked sequentially ('threaded') to the original posting. Participants in this community can respond to any of the messages in a thread – the original message or subsequent replies.

When I thought about the topic of building virtual team capability, I felt it might be appropriate to give people time to share, reflect, and build on each other's ideas, so I created a threaded discussion. Here's my original message:

Posted by: Will Williams
Date posted: Mon 6 November 10.35
Subject: Building virtual team capabilities
Message:
As many of you already know, I am briefing SHE for her TV appearance re: the new workplace. My specific topic in this

forum is developing and making the best use of the knowledge, skills, and experiences of distributed team members to
produce best results. I'll close the discussion on 20 November, synthesize the thinking into a Wiki document and put
it up for your review and editing.

And so it begins.

BIRTH OF A NEW AGE

Early this afternoon my Instant Message alert dinged. It was
Robert Chang from San Francisco.

Robert: Hello Will. Got a minute.

Will: Yes, sure. Good to meet u.

Robert: U2.

Will: How's San Fran?

Robert: Not sure. Am in Delivery Room with wife,
Sally. Labor goes on and on. Doc says getting
closer, but I need to do something productive
right now.

Will: You're able to get online in the hospital. What about
electronic interference?

Robert: Doctor is a good friend. I set up his wireless system
at home. He owes me ;)

Will: Hmm ... maybe u should just focus on Sally.

Robert: No prob. She's messaging with friends between
contractions. Wired world Will – continuous connectivity, pervasive computing and all that.

Will: Yes, but ... .

Robert: Got a camera hooked up to PC. Hold on. I'll show
you what's going on here.

Will: Noooooooooo thx. Give best to wife tho.

Robert: Suit yerself Will. Fascinating stuff. Miracle of life
etc. ☺

Will: Sadie over here in UK said u r a great virtual team
leader. If time, any insights?

Robert: Sadie's terrific. Hold on Will ... no, false alarm ... it was just gas, I think.

Will: Oooh. Maybe you should really focus on your wife.

Robert: She's fine. Virtual team leadership ... let me think. I once did a presentation on that. Yes, I remember, I talked about the virtual team leader's job as being to Energize, to Enable, and to Empower.

Will: Can you explain that if you've still got time.

Robert: Sure. It's difficult to stay motivated and feel like a team when you're virtual so a key role of the virtual leader is to keep energizing team members. Hang on Will, my wife is trying to say something ... she just needs some water. Nurse has gone to get it.

Will: Are you really sure you should be doing this now?

Robert: It's easy to lose energy on a virtual team because of things like distance, gaps in communication, and not feeling you know what's going on. So, the leader has got to be regularly pumping up the team or the energy will leak out of it.

Will: You mean, be a cheerleader?

Robert: Well ... not really. I think teams who are together for a while become tired and cynical if the leader is always waving virtual pom poms around and screaming and yelling from the sidelines. No, I think it's subtler than that.

Will: Tell me more?

Robert: I was afraid you'd ask me that. ... You've got to be a presence to everyone most of the time so that you act as a stable reference point, and you also need to be feeding the virtual space with energizers.

Will: ??????

Robert: Reward and recognition are obvious ones, but I've also been surprised how energizing plain old inter-action and information can be. Updates on how the team is doing in relation to goals, helping the team see the big picture, discussing overall strategy, letting them know other things being done outside the team. I make sure I also talk to team members even when I don't have to. Be right back Will. They want me to fetch the water this time.

Will: Are things still OK there? Do you still have time?

Robert: I'm back. Nothing major going on … . The leader also has to enable the team to do what it needs to do. Make sure there is clarity around goals, expectations, roles and responsibilities, processes, etc. Also help remove barriers, ensure resources are available, and help establish team norms. The leader is responsible for creating the conditions for team success. Hang on Will. … They want me to give Sally some gas and air. …

Will: If you insist!

Robert: OK, things are relatively calm again. The last one is to empower people. On a virtual team the leader is primarily a facilitator, by necessity. You're deluded if you think you can command a virtual team. Distance and time mean you have to operate through developing trust and empowering others to share leadership responsibilities. Know where your people's strengths are and identify capabilities they want to develop. You can't be everywhere you'd like to be. The leader facilitates the team in establishing guidelines, protocols, and parameters. … Hang on again Will, more gas and air.

Will: Maybe you could e-mail me something when you're not so … you know.

Robert: Hold on Will. More gas … no, no … wait, this is getting exciting. Yes. We're really pushing! Woooohoooo. Are you sure you don't want me to turn the camera on?

Will: No, no. Thx anyway. We'll chat again.

THREADING OUR WAY

When I arrived this morning, I checked the Forum. There were two replies to my posting:

Posted by: Sunil Mehta, Bangalore
Date posted: Tues 7 November 08.37
Subject: Team Capability
Message:

Very glad to see the work is still in progress William, and I'm also pleased to see you give 'knowledge' a prominent place in your description of virtual team capability. When exploring team capability, we need to think at two levels. First, the team level – how robust are the processes and systems the team has for generating, sharing, and applying knowledge? The second is the individual level – what are the mindsets, areas of expertise, skills, and experiences that can be leveraged by the team? Teams, whether they are face-to-face or virtual, are knowledge-processing organisms. They feed on data and information that they transform into knowledge for application in activities like product development, marketing strategies, etc. Supporting the processing and application of knowledge are the 'hard' and 'soft' skills individuals bring. On the 'hard' side, for example, there are skills like project management, finance, and IT. On the 'soft' side there are skills like relationship management and communication. When we talk about team capability, we need to think about strengthening those factors – 'hard' and 'soft', team and individual – that help put collective knowledge and know-how to work.

Posted by: Emily Wagner, Chicago
Date posted: Tues 7 November 14:42
Subject: Team Capability
Message:

I agree with Sunil that business teams are knowledge-processing organisms (although I think the language he uses is a leftover from his consulting days – sorry Sunil, you know

I love you!). To keep it simple, I have a few questions posted on my bulletin board:

Team Expertise (Knowledge, Skills, and Experience)

- Who on the team has it, if anyone?
- Who can get it?
- Who can create it?
- Who wants to learn it?
- Who needs it?
- Who is best to share it and keep it updated?
- Who can build on it?
- Who can make it usable?
- Who can best apply it?

While there were only two postings, I felt it was a solid and useful start. Hopefully, more will follow.

MAGICAL THINKING

Moonbeam came to me at lunch today with what she called her 'wicked plan'. She had once told me that she was descended from the Pendle witches who became famous in Lancashire in the early seventeenth century. She added that when she isn't randomizing files in the name of complexity theory, she dabbles in the dark arts. Nothing serious, just casting the evil eye on those she finds truly obnoxious, and working some evenings on a psychic telephone hotline.

Moonbeam, it seems, has warm feelings toward Webster 'The Bugster' Rushkoff. She wants to get to know him better, to cast the 'love eye' on him. As part of getting to know him she plans to set up her video camera overnight and film him while he works (he doesn't appear to go home). She feels that by watching the video again and again she will be able to channel his mind and trigger loving feelings in her direction. It's a theory!

She's telling me this because it will only work if someone born under the sign of Libra (that's me) also participates. She had found out my birth sign by chance when my personnel file 'emerged' from her Office Supplies folder. I told her I didn't feel particularly good about being lost in Office Supplies, but she ignored me. Apparently, just knowing about her plan means I have participated! I asked her why she didn't just talk to him, but she said where's the fun in that?

THREADING OUR WAY AGAIN

There was a very interesting posting when I checked this morning.

> **Posted by:** Diceman
> **Date posted:** Wed 10 November 23:26
> **Subject:** Team Capability
> **Message:**

You know I always think in terms of games, so when I saw Will's posting I imagineered some kind of Knowledge Labyrinth game. Check it out.

In the game, I see members of a team entering a dark labyrinth from different doorways. At the centre of the labyrinth is the team's goal (their Quest). There are multiple roles to be played by team members to reach the goal effectively. Each team member will be dealt several role and knowledge 'cards' that help in reaching the goal. The knowledge is distributed among the team so they must collaborate to succeed. A team member cannot achieve the goal on his or her own. Are you with me so far?

I imagine two sets of roles. I call the first set the **DISTURBERS:**

Questioners – those who ask what, why, where, who, when, and how?

Originators – those who innovate and generate new knowledge.

Transformers – those who take existing knowledge and build on it.

Seekers – those who are hunters and gatherers for knowledge to help in the quest.

Experimenters – those who try new things and learn from them.

The second set I call the **MOBILIZERS**:

Accelerators – those who speed up the transfer of knowledge to where it needs to be.
Amplifiers – those who make 'noise' to make sure people are paying attention.
Distributors – those who create and service the channels through which knowledge flows.
Coordinators – those who identify and forge links between different areas of knowledge.
Implementers – those who apply the knowledge to produce a desired result.
Multipliers – those who use the knowledge to generate new possibilities.
Prioritizers – those who help team members stay focused on what is critical.
Sense Makers – those who promote understanding of the knowledge through interpretation and translation.
Validators – those who test the knowledge to see if it is good.

Man, I like this! Next we would need to create Levels of Expertise for team members like Novice, Practitioner, and Expert. Obviously those at Practitioner and Expert levels can do more things, but they must make sure the Novices keep gaining knowledge and power, and that they don't get lost in the journey. Novices must grow to keep adding strength to the team.

In undertaking their quest, the team members would have to face and overcome the **DESTRUCTORS** – rabid beasts that wander through the labyrinth seeking to damage the capability of the team in reaching its goal. Perhaps someone else could think about what the DESTRUCTORS would be. It's late here. I also need to pump the bilges in the houseboat; water looks deeper than usual down there. Sayonara.

HELP ME OBIWAN

Remember Paula, the psychotic journalist? She's emailed me again! She's got nerve, I'll give her that, but she's a complete delusional: *Will, you've had your chance and now I've moved on. Someone else has come into my life, and you're not half the man that he is. Paula*

What is she talking about? What twisted fantasy has she woven in her head about us? When I told my sister Bess, she just said, 'Doesn't the term *sociopath* mean anything to you? Stay out of her way, brother!' Well, that seems to be easier said than done.

I Googled sociopath. I had a chuckle to myself when I thought I might come across an ad saying 'Sociopath: Find what you want on E-Bay', but I didn't.

ONCE MORE UNTO THE THREADS

A few more threads in the Forum today.

Posted by: Keiko, Tokyo
Date posted: Mon 13 November 06:30
Subject: Teamworks
Message:
Excuse English please. Hope meaning is clear though. I am thinking if knowledge key to success of team – and no doubt it – is important for team to know something about types which it might existence come. From examples, knowledge could be tacit (I have heard term) among team members. Peoples take granted knowledge they have. Is necessary to make naked expert knowledge. Other knowledges are open for all; I think explicit is term. Also good knowing knowledge existing in team, and new knowing needed to get goal. Also good knowing if knowledge OK specific or should be common all. Thank you again for my English.

Posted by: Daavid Gustafsson, Helsinki
Date posted: Mon 13 November 14:22

Subject: Processes
Message:

Really appreciate your input Keiko. Keiko is right about
the value of a team understanding more about 'knowledge'
and how different forms might help or hinder the team.
I'm always surprised how little we know about what we
know, and how we know it. It's important to think about
the processes by which knowledge on the team can be
uncovered, discovered, shared, adapted, absorbed, and put
to work. There aren't any really structured processes in *The
Fun House* to do those things. We find and build our capabilities by accident rather than design. How can we increase
the sharing of best practices in the *House* in a more rigor-
ous way?

Posted by: Alain Badeau, Paris
Date posted: Tues 14 November 09:40
Subject: Processes
Message:

I am pleased for Daavid to open up discussion on processes. I don't so much like idea of best practices. What is
best practice for Daavid in Finland could be worst practice
for me in France. We must understand the context in which
the practice is 'best' or else we risk imposing stupid practices.
Practices must be negotiated to fit each case. We must
precise our understanding of best practice.

Posted by: Daavid Gustafsson, Helsinki
Date posted: Tues 14 November 11:10
Subject: Processes
Message:

Alain makes a good point, but I think in *The Fun
House* we keep reinventing the wheel – as the English
say. That's just too inefficient. Not every situation is totally
unique (even in France). I think we can benefit across the
team if we are clear about some key capability-building
processes like how we create new ideas, how we research

those ideas, how we develop knowledge around those ideas, and share and retain the knowledge not just within the team but across teams. Knowledge can be one-off or re-usable, and we should be paying close attention to what can be reused.

Posted by: Alain Badeau
Date posted: Tues 14 November 13:07
Subject: Taking Offence
Message:
What do you mean 'even in France'? Sounds insulting. Explain please.

Posted by: Daavid Gustafsson, Helsinki
Date posted: Tues 14 November 15:23
Subject: Taking Offence
Message:
I meant no offence. I had read somewhere about the French liking to focus on the particular, the unique rather than the universal, which is why the French will often say, 'It depends,' when asked a question. Isn't that correct?

Posted by: Alain Badeau
Date posted: Tues 14 November 15:45
Subject: Taking Offence
Message:
It depends, but I think you need to read more sophisticated books about the French and keep your stereotypes under control. What you say is ridiculous, childish.

Posted by: Daavid Gustafsson, Helsinki
Date posted: Tues 14 November 16:30
Subject: Taking Offence
Message:
You're the child for reacting in such a way. Idiotic response.

Posted by: Alain Badeau
Date posted: Tues 14 November 16:45
Subject: Taking Offence
Message:
Are you drunk? I've read that the Finns love to drink themselves stupid! There, a stereotype back in your face!

Posted by: Sunil Mehta
Date posted: Wed 15 November 08:00
Subject: Taking Offence
Message:
Daavid and Alain. You are both in the grip of what Geoff would call a DESTRUCTOR. Let me call this one the Escalator. Someone takes offence and then offends the other, leading to more retaliation. You both need to step off the escalating spiral, take a few deep breaths, and then solve the problem constructively. Any conflict can be a deep learning experience if you approach it in a problem-solving way. Please, let us continue the dialogue in a spirit of learning from each other.

Posted by: Daavid Gustafsson, Helsinki
Date posted: Wed 15 November 09:03
Subject: Taking Offence
Message:
You're right. Thanks Sunil. Alain, I will call you. This can be dealt with much better on the phone.

Posted by: Alain Badeau
Date posted: Wed 15 November 10:10
Subject: Taking Offence
Message:
I await your call.

SURPRISE!

Moonbeam found me at lunch again today and she was obviously troubled. She had carried out her plan to video

'The Bugster', but she was now faced with unintended consequences. Bugs had actually untangled himself from his semi-fetal position in front of his monitor and left at 6:45 pm. At 7:00 pm, Mitchell Crabtree appears on camera. The quality is not very good, but Crabtree is definitely recognizable. I'm not going to describe what he appears to be doing on the tape, except that he seems to be doing it while sitting at Moonbeam's desk. It seems to be an exotic dance of love. I never knew that old G&D, who coughs his blackened lungs over his spreadsheets each day, could possibly raise that level of energy. If the attentions of Crabtree weren't bad enough for Moonbeam to endure, the boyfriend she is currently going out with saw the video and demands to know *who* the old geezer is on it and why *she* has it? Who are these perverts she's hanging about with when she's not with him? If Moonbeam doesn't tell him, he's going to download it on to *YouTube* and have the world see what goes on at *The Fun House.*

'It's virtually blackmail,' said Moonbeam.

'Virtual being an appropriate word here,' I replied. 'What are you going to do?'

'I don't know,' she whimpered, 'it's all gone horribly wrong. If I dump my boyfriend he'll download the video for sure. If I tell him it was Crabtree, he'll probably beat him up, and I wouldn't want that on my conscience.' Arthur (the boyfriend) works out a lot and is into extreme kickboxing.

I couldn't think of anything for Moonbeam to do but procrastinate. Distract the boyfriend as much as possible until the emotional energy has seeped out of the situation. She said she would try that.

'But in the meantime,' she continued, 'I have to work in the same building as that creep, and sit at my desk where he's been! Yuck, and double yuck! Doesn't he have a wife and grown-up children?'

Someone said to me once that character is what you do when other people aren't watching. I like that, and it's so critical in a virtual workplace where people aren't watching you all the time. Not that I want to sound self-righteous and full of myself. I have flaws – not exactly sure what they are ... joking! And what about privacy? Enough thinking, there's work to be done.

CONTINUOUS THREADS

Posted by: Rosemary Keital, New York
Date posted: Thur 16 November 11:37
Subject: Knowledge Labyrinth
Message:

I *loved* the Diceman's Knowledge Labyrinth idea and have been thinking about the DESTRUCTORS. Here's a few from my experience to add to Sunil's **Escalator**:

Hoarders – gremlins that lock up knowledge and skills; often a way of keeping power or protecting status.

Charlatans – those who pretend they have knowledge and skills but really don't; you put your trust in them and they don't deliver.

Chaotics – those who have little discipline or ability to organize their work.

Blockers – those who like to put barriers in the way such as 'Can't be done'.

Toxics – those whose attitudes and behaviours destroy any motivation to cooperate, e.g. those who take credit for other people's work, those who have no enthusiasm or energy for what they are doing, cynics, egotists, hypercompetitors, pessimists, the volatiles, the 'my-way or no-wayers', the deceivers who will lie to protect themselves, the avoiders who use distance to shirk responsibilities, and the well-breds who will just tell you what they think you want to hear.

Whirling Dervishes – those who cannot stay focused on priorities and spin out of control.

I'm sure others can add more to my list. If the Labyrinth was a game, team members would pick from a pile of cards in each round and either get a Knowledge Card or if they're unlucky a DESTRUCTOR Card, which might mean penalties for them and/or the team as a whole.

Posted by: Alice Evans, London
Date posted: Thur 16 November 17:12
Subject: Another Viewpoint
Message:
Have been reading the discussion with great interest (apart from Daavid's and Alain's little spat). It seems to me that the important focus should be on the interactions of the team and whether or not they enable or disable knowledge generation, flow, and application. The interactions I'm thinking of are:

People–People – how do we ensure people are willing and able to exchange their expertise?

People–Technologies – how do we ensure people are proficient in using our technologies, and that each one can use the right technology for the right job?

People–Ideas – how do we ensure people are willing and able to contribute their ideas, and in a way that others can easily understand and apply? How do we ensure we can tap into the valuable ideas from the past?

People–Processes – how do we ensure people are comfortable with the formal and informal ways the team operates?

People–Environments – how do we ensure people interact effectively and get value from the contexts in which they work, e.g. team, local, company, and industry environments?

Posted by: Alain Badeau, Paris
Date posted: Sat 18 November 08:45
Subject: Another Viewpoint
Message:
What Daavid and I had was not a 'little spat' as you call it. How people talk to one another is part of the People–People interactions. It is important, not at all trivial.

Posted by: Alice Evans, London
Date posted: Sat 18 November 09:05

Subject: Another Viewpoint
Message:
You're right Alain. I apologize.

Posted by: Sunil Mehta, Bangalore
Date posted: Sat 18 November 18:16
Subject: Another Viewpoint
Message:
That's excellent Alice. The interactions you talk about relate, in my view, to the Team Level capabilities I introduced earlier. These are questions the whole team needs to address. That still leaves the level of individual capabilities.

LUNCH WITH SADIE AND ALICE EVANS

Sadie invited me for lunch along with Alice of 'little spat' fame. Sadie had a feeling that I would get along with Alice (I haven't told Sadie about Sophie, yet). Alice was intelligent, and, yes, very attractive. (I'm sorry if saying that isn't PC, but I can't suddenly switch off the fact that I'm a male. I can control how I behave towards her – respectfully – but I can't control my thoughts. I'm not the Dalai Lama! At least not in this lifetime.)

Alice's mother is Cambodian and her father Welsh. He had met her on a back-packing trip to the temples of Angkor Wat. Alice has a lovely mix of accents that made me want to keep her talking. While I tried to keep the conversation social, it inevitably drifted to my workplace project.

'Unlike Sadie, I love working virtually,' said Alice. Sadie pulled a face and rolled her eyes, but Alice wasn't going to be deterred. 'At my last job before *The Fun House*, my manager, like Sunil, was an ex-consultant. He always had a bag of tricks for every occasion. At one of our team meetings he introduced us to what he called his TRADITIONS framework; it's a bit ironic really when you consider it's about the capabilities people need in working in the new workplace.'

'Consultants drive me crazy,' interrupted Sadie. 'Don't they have anything better to do than sit around and think up these stupid acronyms? I bet they all laugh at us mere mortals as they deposit their cheques and head off to the beach.'

'Sadie, I never knew you are such a cynic!' retorted Alice. 'Some of the things they do can be useful.'

'Really. Consultants are in the top five of my Most Useless People list,' said Sadie. 'I'll show it to you sometime Will. You have a place of honour,' she said smiling. I ignored the tease and let Alice continue.

'The first part of it is Technological Competence; you're not going to help the team in any way if you're not comfortable with the technologies. Most of our generation is OK with the technology, but that doesn't make us good virtual team players.'

'Next is Results-Orientation. ...'

'Wait,' said Sadie, 'are you going to go through all of the TRADITIONS stuff, right now? I've got a conference call with the States in 20 minutes.' Alice looked at me for guidance and I looked at Sadie.

'Why don't I just tell you what each part stands for and then you can ask me questions,' offered Alice.

'Sounds good to me,' I said.

'OK, here goes – Technological Competence, Results-Orientation, Accountability, Discipline, Interpersonal Awareness, Time Management, Initiative, Openness, Networking, and Self-Sufficiency.'

'It feels comprehensive,' I said, 'and even though Sadie might kick me, can you just give me short explanations?' Sadie did kick me (close to where Paula had spiked me with her stiletto), but luckily she had taken her shoes off when she sat down.

'OK, speed explanations,' said Alice, taking a big breath. 'All the members must feel everyone is committed and being accountable otherwise the team can fall apart quickly. Without self-discipline, routines, and good organizational skills your virtual experience can get really ugly. You'll create your own chaos and that chaos will spread like a virus.'

'Even quicker,' urged Sadie tapping on her watch. Alice paused for another large intake of breath.

'Everyone needs good interpersonal awareness to develop and keep good relationships, and you must manage your time carefully and set personal boundaries otherwise constant interruptions and demands will drive you crazy.'

Pause for deep breath.

'You've got to be able to take the initiative and not be waiting around for permission, and being open is critical to learning from others.'

Pause for another deep breath.

'Networking is obviously important for staying connected and building resources. And last, self-sufficiency – you've got to be very secure and confident in working alone and being able to manage ambiguity and uncertainty. Whew!' Sadie and I both applauded, while Alice made a mock bow and wiped her brow.

'I'm not really good at dealing with ambiguity and uncertainty,' said Sadie. 'I like certainty. Isn't that right Will?' I couldn't miss the cutting reference to my own inability to provide her with certainty in our relationship. I wasn't done hearing Alice's lovely voice so I asked her another question. 'So what's been your worst virtual team experience?'

'Oh, that would have to be the *Dark Matter* team which crashed and burned about 18 months ago.'

Sadie, who had her own experiences with the *Dark Matter* team, choked violently on her food and projected substantial chunks of cold sesame noodle on to the Sudoku puzzle of an elegant women sitting at the next table (what is it with Sadie and her inability to keep food to herself?). The poor woman turned pale green, then deep purple, and then ashen. I thought she was going to be violently sick, but she managed to maintain a dignified, if wobbly, presence. Sadie apologized profusely while a waiter rushed over and scraped the offending food off the puzzle and into an ice bucket. I've missed another *YouTube* moment I cursed; another lost opportunity for Internet celebrity.

The waiter ushered us quietly out of the restaurant, with Sadie continuing to apologize and offering to buy the woman another Sudoku book.

'Did you see the colours that poor woman turned?' said Alice.

'Just pigments of your imagination,' I said, unable to resist a pun. Sadie and Alice shook their heads and walked on in front of me. When they reached the curb, Sadie looked back at me and said, 'Me and Daniel want you to come over for a meal Friday night. Seven o'clock, and bring a friend if you like,' she said her head nodding in Alice's direction.

Oh no … no more complications in my life. Why couldn't I have told Sadie about Sophie? Also, I'd have to go and witness the domestic bliss of Daniel and Sadie; I really didn't want to be tortured with that, but I didn't see a way out.

CAN YOU FETCH YOUR FATHER?

'Darling.'

'Yes, Mother?'

'Your foolish father has got himself into trouble with the police,' she said bitterly.

'What do you mean?'

'Well he parked his van somewhere alongside the River Severn near Shrewsbury and slept in it. Sometime during the night he left the van and wandered into the town in his underwear.'

'What? You mean he was sleepwalking?'

'Who knows what that eccentric old fool was doing? His mind is a mystery to me. He couldn't even show the police where he'd parked the van. They decided he wasn't drunk, drugged, or a danger to anyone. Anyway, they want someone to fetch him and move the van.'

'And you would like me to do that?'

'Yes, be a darling. I am so busy with rehearsals and can't possibly get away.'

'O … K.'

'You're a darling, an absolute angel.'

On the train up to Shrewsbury I listened to *MIA* at full volume. There was a group of raucous, foul-mouthed school kids on the train; I kept my eyes averted and thought about the sorrowful state of England's future – if these kids were any indicator. Then I considered with some alarm the awful prospect that perhaps I was getting old!

COMMUNICATION

NISHA'S THOUGHT FOR THE DAY

In Nisha's most recent Clog entry she said: 'I am convinced that the success of not only our business, but of all human-kind, lies in the quality of the conversations we have with one another – face-to-face and virtually. If we were able to teach our children only one thing, it should be how to talk to one another constructively, in a spirit of mutual learning, and with respect.' I like Nisha, and not just for her Chicken Makani.

OUT OF THE MOUTHS OF BABES

Seb, my nephew, is wicked with words. I remember visiting Bess and family one raw October day. Seb and Em were playing hide and seek outside, while we sensible adults huddled around a paraffin heater drinking hot chocolate. Seb suddenly burst through the door holding up his frozen hands and screaming, 'I'm so ice-so-lated.' Wonderful! One day he said to his grandmother, 'You can't help me with this puzzle 'cause you've got gastromentalitis!' Communication can be a lot of fun if you're not working with someone a million miles away and frantically trying to meet a killer deadline.

NO, NO YOU MISUNDERSTAND ME

I've had an interesting exchange over the last couple of days. I had been instant messaging with Rodrigo Gomez in Mexico about sales figures from the Latin American region. We got on well and chatted as best we could about football and films. At the end of the chat I wrote, 'Thanks Rodrigo. Take care.'

The next day Rodrigo called me: 'Will, tell me as a friend, do you know something that I don't know. Is my performance too bad? Am I losing my job?'

I was stunned. 'Rodrigo, who did you hear that from?'

'From you, Will.'

'What! I never said anything about you being a bad performer or losing your job!'

'I heard it, Will. I heard it from you. You told me to "Take care", but what have I done to deserve this?'

I didn't get it at first, but then I realized he thought I was warning him that something bad was about to happen and that he should be careful.

'No Rodrigo, you misunderstood. All I meant was for you to look after yourself. Sorry, that's not helping. "Take care" is simply a polite way to end a conversation. I suppose it means that I care about you.'

'You are telling me that you are gay?'

'No Rodrigo. I'm not gay. I was simply being polite. Like if I said "Have a nice day" at the end of our conversation.'

'You are a gay American?'

'No Rodrigo, I'm neither. Please listen carefully. …'

I eventually cleared up the misunderstanding and Rodrigo was relieved to hear that he was not losing his job. The exchange was a reminder that communication is so much more than exchanging words. Communication only happens when *meanings* are shared. Tricky.

NIGHTMARE

My father hadn't been in a good state when I picked him up from Shrewsbury police station. He was disoriented and desperate looking. The police had retrieved some clothes from his van and given him a blanket, but he still looked like he was freezing inside himself. I got him back to his van in a taxi and then drove him home. I kept asking what had happened, but he couldn't tell me. He just stared out of the van window at the winter fields.

He's a good man, my father, even though he has his eccentricities. Before he retired his pupils had adored him. He could make history come alive with the way he told stories. When he described Cicero speaking in the Roman Senate or Caesar defeating the army of Pompey at the battle of Pharsalus, you felt like you were there. Words to him were more than packets of information; they were fabulous treasures with meaning and power. I wish more people in cyberland, or in any land, felt the same way.

I woke up panicked this morning, soaked in sweat and with tears pouring down my face. Sophie held me and wanted to know what was wrong. In my dream, I had seen my father standing alone in the middle of a winter field holding out his arms to me, terrified and frightened. The word pile-driving into my head was Alzheimer's! God, it can't be. Not that. Was my father going to disappear into a place where I couldn't reach him or him me?

HAVING A LAUGH

Sometimes my joking gets in the way of communicating. I know it does, but I can't seem to stop myself. Take this morning, for example, when Aki Kwon from Hong Kong pinged me with an instant message:

Aki: Hi Will, I'm here. Are you?
Will: No, I'm here.
Aki: I don't understand.
Will: I'm not where you are, but where I am.
Aki: Where?
Will: Here.
Aki: But I thought you weren't here.
Will: I'm not.

Aki: Can we start again please?
Will: From where?
Aki: Do you have 5 minutes to chat?
Will: With you or with anyone?
Aki: I will chat with you when there is a better mood.
Will: But I'm in a great mood.
Aki: I think you are making fun of my English perhaps.

I tried to keep chatting with her, but she went silent. I was only giving her what we call in Britain 'a hard time' – just joking with her. Think I'll have to do some repair work with Aki.

Before leaving for the night, I thought about Theresa, SHE's sister. She is one of the smartest people I've met – at least in relation to the digital workplace – so on my way home I sent her a quick e-mail to see if she would meet with me to talk about virtual communication. She agreed to meet later in the week at a pub I know in Islington. It's not far from where both Theresa and Sophie live. I could meet Sophie afterwards for a curry.

IN *THE WIT'S END CAFÉ*

This afternoon, I poured myself a cup of coffee and went into *The Wit's End Café* on GO*dz*W*illa* (the rule is that you don't go into *The Wit's End* unless you have something *real* to drink – tea, coffee, juice, water, etc.). A series of random words like *Indifference, Wisdom, Foreigner, Asymmetrical,* and *Breakout* came up over random photos of inner-city scenes, paintings and sculptures, archeological relics, pictures from the Hubble telescope, and circus performances. It was aimed at creating a surreal experience for supporting creativity. I was enjoying the down-time for a couple of minutes when I noticed that someone else was in the café – Karl Schafer in Berlin. I decided to chat with him.

Will: Hello Karl.

Karl: Yes. Who are you?

Will: Will Williams in London.

Karl: Yes, I read your name, but *who* are you?

Will: Philosophically, that's a very tough question to answer.

Karl: I have no time for jokes please. *How* can I help you?

Will: Just thought we could chat for a minute about working across distances.

Karl: I have a meeting in 7 minutes.

Will: I'll be quick. Do you do a lot of work virtually?

Karl: Virtually? Do you mean do I *almost* work?

Will: No, no. Do you do a lot of work with people in other parts of the world via technology?

Karl: Why do you ask me this?

Will: I'm doing an assignment on how well we work virtually in *The Fun House*.

Karl: How do you intend to use this information?

Will: Just generally. I won't be using any names. I saw you in the café and just thought I would ask your opinion.

Karl: I see. I am not so keen on what you call this virtual work.

Will: Really. Why not?

Karl: I think too many people take advantage.

Will: In what way?

Karl: Because we are not face-to-face, some people find it easy to make promises and not keep them. I have been let down several times, and put in difficult situations. I think in America they call these people *Freeriders*. I do not like these people. I try to start on a team with a positive frame of mind, but until I see others delivering on what they have promised I am skeptical.

Will: You find it hard to trust until people have actually performed?

Karl: Yes. That is what I am telling you. What is worse is when people give the impression they are with you 100 percent, but the collaboration amounts to nothing; it is meaningless. Often, I think they do not read what I send, otherwise they would not ask such stupid questions. I call them *Teasers*.

Will: You have strong feelings about this.

Karl: Of course. I call them, and others like them, virtual vandals.

Will: Others?

Karl: Yes. There are the *Psychics* who think you can read their minds, and that they can read yours. So much time is wasted in clearing up the misunderstandings or filling in gaps. There are also the *ODs* or *One-Dimensionals*; these people use the same method for communicating absolutely everything, usually e-mail, regardless of how suitable it is. But I must go.

Before I could thank him he signed out of the café. Those virtual vandals sounded like blood relations to the Destructors in Diceman's Knowledge Labyrinth game.

SOME EXPLAINING TO DO

I met Theresa in the Islington pub and we found a corner away from the arcade games and the football on TV (my team was losing away from home, again!). She looked anxious, but after a few mouthfuls of a Cosmopolitan cocktail she brightened up.

'Thanks for the invite, Will. I needed a change of scene,' she said softly.

'I knew when I wanted to learn more about virtual communication, you would be the right person to ask.'

'I'm flattered,' she said, giving me that summer smile I am so used to seeing with SHE. 'What can I help you with?'

'Can we talk about the challenges of virtual communication and some possible solutions?'

'Sounds good.' She gulped another mouthful of her Cosmopolitan before continuing. 'I think we can categorize the challenges as Too Much and Too Little.'

She picked up her drink glass and massaged it between her hands while I waited. Her eyes panned over the night skies outside, and I could tell she was struggling to surmount a wall of sadness. 'OK ... Well, alright then,' I laughed. 'Thanks for coming and sharing your expertise with me.' Jokingly, I stood up to leave. She giggled and pulled me back down on to the chair beside her.

'Oh Will, you do make me laugh. Thanks for that ... where was I? Right, Too Much and Too Little. Let's think about Too Much first.' She downed her drink very quickly and indicated that she would like another one before going on. When I returned, she took another large gulp and started up the conversation again.

'I said that the challenges are related to Too Much and Too Little, but what I didn't say was that I see the solutions in two sets also: Technology and Behaviour.' She pulled a mechanical pencil out of her bag and drew four quadrants on the back of a beer mat.

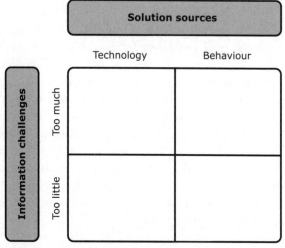

Information challenges and solution sources.

'I think you'll find most of the challenges and solutions are in those four boxes,' she said taking another slug of her drink.

'Well, there's nothing in there right now. Are you going to give me any clues?' I laughed, 'or is there a consultant fee for the rest?'

'Well, there's also nothing more in here,' she said pointing to her glass, and directing me towards the bar for another. Whoa, take it easy Theresa, I thought. The surly barman whose thick arms were corkscrewed with snake tattoos asked me if my lady friend was planning to remain in the world of the living or drink her way to paradise.

'Too much,' Theresa said loudly when I returned to our quiet alcove. 'We all know about information overload. Our technologies are outpacing our abilities to process all this information. Some people get a buzz out of receiving 300 e-mails a day. I suppose it makes them feel they are the centre of the universe, but you can't be effective when your mind is scattered so thinly. I know other people who will go online and print off hundreds of articles related to a problem they have to solve. But they often drown themselves in information and either suffer analysis paralysis or stop thinking for themselves.'

'Ah, you know me so well,' I tittered. Theresa smiled and took a large swig of her latest Cosmo. 'So what do we do?' I asked.

'As I mentioned earlier, we need to look for solutions in Technology and Behaviour. We can get technology to do some sorting and filtering for us by enabling the software to learn about our wants, needs, and priorities and make suggestions – you know, personalized searching. We can also have other people help us by tagging their favourites.'

She stopped to down her drink before continuing on. 'We need to get better at using the technology to do the work of finding and prioritizing. Put the technology to work, Will.'

'What about behaviour?' I asked.

'I think that is the biggest challenge right now, and I think a lot of it has to do with establishing routines, protocols, and discipline.'

As before, Theresa stopped talking, massaged her glass, and stared into space.

'You said the other challenges were related to Too Little,' I prompted.

'Yes I did, didn't I, and you probably want to know more don't you. Well, that will cost you another Cosmo.' I came back with another Cosmo, and also some packets of peanuts and potato crisps that I piled in the middle of the table. I had the sneaking suspicion she hadn't eaten food since lunchtime, maybe breakfast, and was drinking on an empty stomach. 'My Will, you really know how to win a woman's heart,' she said looking at the mound of nuts and crisps. 'Are you trying to seduce me?'

It took more than a little subtle guiding, but I managed to get Theresa back to talking about the challenges of virtual communication.

'The problem of Too Little is as big a problem as Too Much. Virtual communication is often said to be too impersonal. As a consequence, a lot of people say it is very inferior to face-to-face communication, but I think it's just a different form. When writing and posting letters was developed some people may have thought the method was too impersonal and was the end of *real* human relationships. But we know that wasn't true. I have online chats with friends and it feels as warm and intimate as can be. I think some people are able to open up more when they are not face-to-face. It's not the technologies that are impersonal, but how we use them. The act of trying to communicate is a performance in which we connect with others and work at creating shared meaning. Most of the time we focus on transferring the content and neglect the performance that breathes life into the content.'

'What else do we have too little of in virtual communication?' I said.

'Sometimes, I find context is missing so I can't interpret a message very well. I know Americans, in particular, like the short, sharp e-mail with just a few bullet points. Their presentations tend to be the same – context free.

'When working virtually, we must provide people with whatever background information they need to make sense of what we are saying, writing, or doing. Sometimes less is not more, but not enough. When people are given gaps, they fill them with what makes sense to them, which is often wide of the mark. You can't always know what they need, but you can take an empathic leap.'

'Anything else?'

'I think virtual communication is often lacking in frequency. Some people are left alone too long without knowing what is going on. I also find that some team leaders only communicate with the team as a whole, and individuals feel neglected. We all want to feel listened to and valued. Don't we, Will?'

'Is that it?'

'No. Let me leave you with one more. There is often too little insight. What counts is not the volume of information or data we have, but the learning, the critical insights, the hidden connections, the trends. Web 3.0 or the Semantic Web is expected to support the teasing out of patterns from the unorganized data. Right now, when you do a search, you end up with a slew of documents that may or may not provide an answer to your question. What if the Web acted more like a smart database that organized and drew conclusions from the mass of online bits and bytes?'

'And in terms of behaviours?'

'Right now, I think we are all in the hunting and gathering mindset when we go on the Web. Some thinking might be involved, but it's mostly superficial. I'd like us to gather less and think more. We need to move into an agricultural phase in which we cultivate cyberland to meet our specific needs and produce more value.'

'Beyond the obvious, do you think working with these technologies changes the way we see and interact with other people?' I asked, hoping another question wouldn't lead to another drink (any more and I would have to take out a loan).

'Hmm. I'll have Paul Thomas call you,' she slurred. 'He's an old friend of mine researching that kind of stuff in Silicon Valley.'

This written version of my conversation with Theresa is actually more articulate than it really was. After the second Cosmo, she wasn't really coordinated in either speech or movement. At one point, the barman came to collect our glasses; he stopped to growl into my ear: 'Listen sunshine, if she vomits all over the wife's new rug, there'll be hell to pay, especially from the missus.' Looking down both he and I noticed that Theresa had already stomped heavily on to some peanut and crisp droppings under the table. I thought it best to bring things to a quick conclusion.

'Theresa, thanks so much,' I said brightly. 'You've been a real help. How's Tomas by the way?' I knew as soon as those last few words had left my mouth that I had stepped into something horrendously smelly and unpleasant. A dark melancholy flooded her eyes and her mouth creased into a pained grimace.

'Oh Will,' she cried pitifully, dropping her head on to my shoulder. I could feel her warm tears seeping through my shirt, and then I heard an unwelcome ripping sound as she tugged despairingly at my sleeve. 'She's absolutely fine – no problem,' I mouthed to the anxious barman and the buffed, tattooed wife who had joined him. Oh lordy, I thought to myself as I stroked her hair and whispered useless things like 'Shh, shh, it'll be alright. You'll see.' It was pure impulse on my part, but as I stroked her hair I also kissed her forehead and rested my head on hers.

At first, given the contorted angle I was sitting in and the relative darkness of the alcove, I didn't recognize the female figure walking slowly towards us. Panic leapt to my throat.

Poor Sophie, obviously in shock and awe, stared feverishly at me, her eyes welling up with tears. Before I could even say 'Sophie, I can ...' she hurtled out of the pub door. What a cruel, venomous twist of fate.

I managed to get Theresa home in a taxi. During the trip, I sent Sophie a text: *Not what u think. It's SHE's sister in need. That's all.* Tomas wasn't at the house, so I made Theresa some coffee and sat and talked with her until she seemed relatively *compos mentis*. Tomas apparently had gone on one of his *disappearances*. Three times before, he had left because marriage was 'too stifling and oppressive'. He needed space in which to let his mind and body channel other feelings and experiences, a space in which his male genius could roam freely.

I just couldn't help a broad smile sneak across my face. 'He calls *it* his male genius?' I asked. Theresa looked at me and nodded, her own face breaking into a smile. Soon the smiles erupted into wild hysterical laughter – throat-grinding, fist-pounding, feet-thumping laughter.

When I left Theresa's, I headed straight for Sophie's place where I knew I had some explaining to do. At first, Sophie wouldn't let me in; she had barricaded her door with a sofa. I stood in the street texting her explanations for an hour and then she allowed me to talk to her on the phone. At 12:30 am, we eventually spoke through her old-fashioned keyhole, and at one in the morning she rolled back the sofa and opened the door. Life is strange. That night we made *love* to each other. Not just sex, I mean *love, love, love*, but you don't need to know any more.

INDABA

You might be wondering what happened to those *Indaba* sessions SHE told me to run when I first started this project. Well ... somehow the name put me off until I realized I could simply call it a web meeting.

We have a policy in *The Fun House* to try and be reasonable when we set up teleconferences or web meetings. We don't want a whole bunch of people around the world having to be on their phones and laptops at two or three in the morning. At first those hours are a kind of fun, macho thing to do, and help demonstrate your undying commitment to the company, but after a while they get very old. What we've tried to do is find out when people like to be available and work within those parameters whenever possible. We also try and Share The Misery (STM as we call it) so that we reallocate early mornings or late nights on a regular basis. We also record teleconferences and web conferences so that those who couldn't attend can listen at another time. Some team members, if unable to attend, will record an audio or video podcast of stuff they want to share.

I knew it was London's turn to be in what we call the Sanity Zone and Asia's turn to be in the Insanity Zone, so I went on to the World Clock on the web, planned the meeting, and sent out an e-mail.

Monday, 20 November
Hello everyone,
I'm going to facilitate a web meeting next Wednesday at 16:00 GMT to discuss virtual communication in The Fun House. Please be prepared to share your thoughts on this important topic.

There was an almost instantaneous response from Berlin:

*Will, when you say **next** Wednesday, do you mean Wednesday of this week or Wednesday of next week? I have been caught out by this mistake before? Anton*

Note to self: be specific. Don't assume shared understanding. As my American friends say, when you assume you make an ASS out of U and ME!

I sent a follow-up e-mail to the team being very specific about the date (not this week, but next week).

OPPORTUNITY KNOCKS

Much to Moonbeam's horror, the exotic dancing Crabtree has asked her out. He put it so nicely to her via e-mail. 'I've got nothing interesting to do on Saturday night. I'm willing to give you the opportunity to make it interesting for me. What time shall we meet?' After watching the video she had made in the office, Moonbeam was expecting some kind of approach from Crabtree. As a consequence, she stayed relatively calm – if you consider slapping and shaking her monitor calm. I thought she was having technical problems until she forwarded Crabtree's e-mail to me. She mailed him back. *Sorry to disappoint, but I don't think my boyfriend would appreciate the three of us going out together.* He wrote back, *Well, how about Sunday, without your boyfriend?* At this point, Moonbeam realized she wasn't being explicit enough and replied, *No, no and no. Take your midlife crisis somewhere else and don't ask me again!* Crabtree had to make sure he had the last word and that he could interpret the outcome as a victory for his own ego: *I was really just playing with your mind. I would absolutely have said no if you'd said yes.*

THE TRUTH WILL SET YOU FREE, MAYBE

I had an early morning teleconference this morning that I took at home. I think others were also at home because there was a lot of flushing of toilets, barking dogs, and children yelling on the line. Some might consider such noises to be unprofessional, but I suppose they are all just a part of the new workplace buzz. I call it Snap, Cackle, and Plop.

I got into the office late with two Caffeine Tornadoes, both for me, but SHE wanted one. *Note to self: still need to find good assertiveness training programme.*

Moonbeam had left a note on my desk, 'Need to see you at lunch time. URGENT.' Over her fried macaroni and cheese and my bowl of tongue-blistering chili, she tells me that procrastination hasn't worked with kickboxing Arthur and that he's becoming more jealous and enraged as each day passes.

'You'll have to tell him who it is,' I say. 'Tell him the truth.'

'But, I can't. Arthur will grind G & D into a pulp."

'Well make up a story,' I say.

'Like what?'

'I don't know. Tell him … tell him poor Crabtree has never been the same since he was in a serious golfing accident and wasn't wearing a helmet. Tell him we keep him on because we've grown to love his little quirks, or because of a government regulation.'

'What government regulation?'

'I don't know! Tell him it's "Love an old geezer week!"'

'That's ageist, and besides I'm not good at telling lies.'

'Would you rather see the video on *YouTube*? Who knows what nasty consequences that would dump on your head?'

'I suppose you're right.'

When I got back from lunch, Crabtree was hovering over Moonbeam's 'Meet me for lunch' note that was still on my desk. He didn't say anything, but he threw me a look aimed at severing my carotid artery. He obviously misinterpreted what's going on – or rather, what's not going on – between Moonbeam and me.

INDABA PART ONE

I had decided to run the meeting with just audio in case a lot of people decided to join and the video became distracting. In actuality, there were six others and myself: Robert Chang and Emily Wagner in the US, the Diceman and me in the UK, Anton Weiss in Frankfurt, Sunil Mehta in Bangalore, and Aki Kwon in Hong Kong (cursing myself, I suddenly remembered that I hadn't yet apologized for giving her a 'hard time').

Before we started, I told the group about my recent 'Take care' experience with Rodrigo. Sunil was delighted because it gave him just the right starting point he was looking for to start the discussion about communication.

'At the heart of communication,' he said very seriously, 'are the encoding and decoding processes. When I create a message, I encode it in symbols, words, pictures, and even gestures or emoticons that help me convey what I want to say. I am constructing the message within my encoding context, my system of meanings. The receiver decodes, or more simply, interprets the message from within his or her system of meanings. Ideally, the decoding or interpretation mirrors exactly the message I wanted to communicate.'

Sunil set up a whiteboard area in the meeting. 'Let's take Will's example,' he said enthusiastically. He drew a diagram on the whiteboard that looked like this:

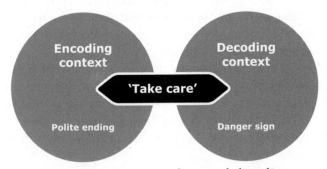

Communication encoding and decoding.

'Will is on the left in his Encoding Context. Rodrigo is on the right in his Decoding Context. Will says "Take care" which in his system of meanings is a polite and caring way to say goodbye. Rodrigo is receiving the message and interpreting it within his system of meanings as a warning. If Rodrigo had not called Will to ask what this warning was about, he could have been in misery for months waiting to lose his job. Luckily, he did call and they could clear up the misunderstanding. Even though we are using English as a common language, do we share a common understanding of the words and phrases we use?'

'This is interesting Sunil,' said Robert, 'but it's a bit theoretical for me. Can we move quicker to what we do now and what we need to do differently?'

'No,' said Anton in Frankfurt abruptly. 'This is useful for me. I need a framework to help me understand. If we rush into dos and don'ts, we will not have a complete picture. I think it is important to ask "why" questions as well as "how".' I had some trouble listening to him, and could feel myself becoming frustrated with his slow pace of speaking and difficulty pronouncing English words. I knew English wasn't his first language, but most Germans I had worked with spoke better English than I did.

While I was thinking these thoughts, I had an IM from Anton:

Anton: Sorry, Will. My technology is not working properly. I will have to sign off.

Will: What's wrong?

Anton: You may know or not know that I am deaf. On my GO*dz*W*illa* I have software that turns speech into text so that I can read what is being said. Right now, it is not working correctly.

Can you imagine what I was feeling at that point? I wanted to die the death of a thousand cuts. I had made the assumption that Anton's English wasn't very good. To be perfectly honest, I'd thought that he probably wasn't very bright and would have little to contribute. I'm pathetic!

Will: Sorry Anton. I'll tell the others and we'll schedule another time.

When the meeting closed, I took another look inside GO*dz*W*illa*. I didn't have a need for its special applications, so I hadn't really noticed them on the system. *Note to self: young Will needs to do some reading on selective perception*. As well as speech into text there was also a facility for translating video and speech into sign language – an avatar appears in the bottom right-hand corner of the screen and signs to the user. For the blind there are text to speech tools, and even voice controlled access to the Internet tools.[21] There are even instant translation tools converting English text and speech into a number of other languages.

COMMUNICATION MATTERS

After the *Indaba* session, Emily pinged me from the US.

Emily: Hi Will. Are you really there? [I remembered the confusion I'd caused with Aki and decided to play it straight.]

Will: I am.

Emily: You sound a bit curt. Are you OK? [I can't win, can I?]

Will: Yes, I'm fine. Really.

Emily: Was a shame the session got cut short. There was something I wanted to share that might be useful.

Will: Great.

Emily: A friend of mine is a training consultant for global teams, and he's giving me some tips on communication. He's OK with me sending these over to you.

Will: Wonderful. I need all the help I can get.

Emily: All I'm sending right now are the main headings. He

---

[21] Computer technologies for supporting the blind and visually impaired, the physically challenged, and the deaf and hearing impaired have made important strides in recent years. The European Community has a policy initiative aiming for an inclusive information society (e-Inclusion). A subset of e-Inclusion is e-Accessibility aimed at ensuring adequate assistive technologies for utilizing the benefits of information and communication technologies.

said he will get short explanations to me in time for your report. Ping me with any questions.

Will: Many thanks Emily. Bye.

The document from Emily was very useful.

Guidelines for Communicating in Global Teams

General

- Create a formal communications plan to generate a 'team rhythm'.
- Encourage informal spontaneity and networking.
- Communicate one-on-one, not just with the whole team.
- Let others know your communication preferences, and find out what they prefer.
- Sort others into circles of contact (daily, weekly, monthly, as needed).
- Add personality, enthusiasm, and warmth to your virtual communications.
- Vary your use of collaborative technologies.

Verbal Communication

- Slow down to help others understand you.
- Give people time to talk without interrupting.
- Give people time to confer with others.
- Keep language as simple as possible.
- Save time and your sanity by doubling your communication efforts.
- Be honest; don't pretend to understand when you don't.
- Pay attention to what is said and not said, and how something is said.
- Ask questions and check for shared meaning.
- Consolidate understanding.
- Make your questions straightforward.

Written Communication

Note: many of the guidelines for verbal communication also apply to writing.

- Explain background and context; don't cause others to second-guess you.
- Be exact; eliminate vague words.
- Keep e-mails, etc., as short as possible, but no shorter.
- Write carefully so that punctuation and spelling convey exactly what you want to say.
- Be restrained in what and how you write.
- Use visual and numerical anchors to reinforce your meaning.
- Look at the feelings and thoughts behind the words.
- Treat written messages as permanent.

SLEEP TIGHT, AND DON'T LET THE TECHNOLOGY BITE

It's my own fault. I'd left my laptop powered up by the bed, and at 2:30 am I received a call on my VoIP system from Paul Thomas, the researcher in California Theresa had mentioned. Sophie jumped out of her skin when the call came through and accidentally elbowed me in the face. This has left me, some would say deservedly so, with a dazzlingly flamboyant black, purple, and yellow left cheek.

'Paul. Good of you to call,' I lied bravely, as Sophie ran into her kitchen to get a bag of ice for my face.

'No problemo. What can I do for you my friend?' My friend! I haven't even spoken to him before!

I gave him a quick overview of the workplace project and told him I was searching for some research on the impact of technology on virtual collaboration. Of course, the *impact* most on my mind at that moment was the injury received as a result of my being called in the middle of the NIGHT!

'Yeah, that's cool,' he said of the project. 'Let me summarize some of the findings because I know it's early or late there; I can never remember which.' He didn't comment on my loud moan of exasperation because he seemed too much into what he wanted to say. 'There are several findings in the research I think it's worth knowing about,' he said with that glittering American enthusiasm that roused my minor prejudices.[22] 'Whether you're talking about audioconferencing, videoconferencing, or computer-mediated communication, the tendency of the people involved is to be less cooperative with those at other locations. Forming negative impressions of others is most likely in audioconferencing.'

I tried to put all of my negative impressions about Paul aside and focus on the job at hand. 'So, it's very important for all team members to be aware of the potential for unwarranted negative impressions?' I said, impressed with myself for being so articulate at 2:30 am, and with a potentially broken jaw!

'Absolutely,' he went on, 'and to take time to get to know one another upfront through pictures and bios, and one-on-one chats as well as team conversations.'

I could see Sophie in the kitchen making tea. She was wearing just a pair of pink and blue striped boxer shorts, and I had the hardest time concentrating on what Paul was saying. I hoped there wasn't going to be a test.

'With these technologies,' he continued, 'there are often fewer clues for guiding our interpretations and interactions with others. Clues that we are being sarcastic or humorous are often weakened so that it is easy for people to misinterpret our intentions. We often don't have the rich benefits provided by facial expressions, gestures, vocal intonations, and verbal and nonverbal signals indicating the degree of someone's understanding.'

Sophie saw me watching her every move and started dancing seductively. She's quiet and shy, but she can be wicked.

---

[22] Paul e-mailed later with the name of a really good book, *The Internet in the Workplace: How New Technology Is Transforming Work,* by Patricia Wallace. It was published by Cambridge University Press in 2004.

Paul went on oblivious to my torment. 'It's often harder communicating via technology to determine power and status, which is not necessarily a bad thing, but it can lead to uncertainty and reduced participation. It's also known that some people lose their inhibitions in virtual space so that they become less sensitive to interpersonal niceties. People working online feel greater anonymity and reduced social pressure; when communicating they can become very blunt and candid, leading to extended *flaming* sessions in which conflicts escalate. I think some devils actually send certain messages as *flamebait* to stir things up.'

'I, for one, would never do such a thing,' I said, with a laugh. Sophie was definitely stirring things up in the kitchen and elsewhere.

'Another interesting finding is that people participating in video, audio, and computer-mediated communication tend to adopt opinions that are towards the extreme or riskier ends of the spectrum. Polarizations occur more often, and so it pays to analyse risks in more detail.'

Sophie had come to sit beside me on the bed and her tongue was exploring my left ear. I know my breathing was becoming faster and heavier because Paul asked me if I suffered from asthma. 'No, I'm fine. You carry on. This is great stuff', I said, trying to pull myself together.

'Something else it's useful to know if you are involved on teams using audio and videoconferencing is that people tend to agree more with those who are in the same room as themselves.'

I wheezed as Sophie's attention shifted away from my ears. To my relief, the kettle also started wheezing, and off she went to brew the tea.

'This has been very enlightening, Paul. I'm sure you're very busy. Thanks again.'

'If I think of anything else I'll e-mail. You take care of that wheezing, you hear.'

Sophie returned with a pot of tea and two mugs.

'I know I'm British,' I said pulling her towards me, 'but a mug of tea is the last thing on my mind.'

INDABA **PART TWO**

The communication *Indaba* group reconnected a few days after the first session. This time we were joined by Zivah Shalev from Israel and Grigory Petrov from Russia.

Robert Chang started the discussion. 'When it comes to virtual teams,' he said, 'I measure everything by three key indicators: levels of Engagement, Cohesion, and Clarity.'

'I know about them Robert,' I interrupted, 'but perhaps you can explain for everyone else what you mean by them, and how they fit with Sunil's Six Cs.'

'Right … good question …. Engagement is the level of emotional involvement and commitment to the work of the team. Distance tends to work against engagement, but it is critical for achieving the highest levels of team performance. When I talk of Cohesion, I am referring to the level the team works together as a unified, coordinated whole. Finally, we have Clarity and this is the level of shared understanding on the team. Cooperation and communication are not just damaged by lack of honesty and hidden agendas; they also collapse through unclear, confusing messages that leave team members in a virtual fog.'

'Thanks Robert. So what is the relationship between those indicators and the Six Cs?'

'I see the Six Cs as the means, and Engagement, Cohesion, and Clarity as the ends. What do you think Sunil?'

'I think that captures it very nicely, Robert.'

'So everything we do in the Six Cs should be contributing to one or more of the ends you've described?' Aki Kwon asked.

'That's right,' said Robert.

Zivah suggested that we break into three online breakout groups. Each group would take one of the indicators and think about communication behaviours that would support its development. Everyone agreed, and we decided to reconvene in 20 minutes.

While we were in our groups, I received a message from the Diceman: *Sorry Will, got to get out. Houseboat appears to be sinking, or failing to rise with the tide as we say around here.*

I tried to message him back but there was no reply and he wasn't answering his mobile. If your boat is sinking probably the last thing on your mind is answering your mobile. What am I saying? Death before a missed call!

When the groups got back together, each one summarized and discussed their findings.

Robert spoke for the small engagement team. 'What we did was to identify a number of categories and discuss those. The first was team input. Team members need to feel what they say and do matters, and that they have personal as well as shared accountability for results.

'Next was team size. We felt it is hard for a large virtual team to develop strong engagement. If a large team is necessary, say over 12 people, we feel it best to create subteams for different aspects of the work. It is easier to communicate and bond with the few rather than the many. Of course, you will still need to bring the whole team together regularly to coordinate what they are doing.

'The third area we talked about was relationships. At the beginning of the team's life it is important to spend time on getting to know each other, and face-to-face if possible. Social networking technologies will now help us start and keep relationships.

'Next was communication itself. We started with the need to develop a regular rhythm for formal communications, but we also thought about the importance of frequent and spontaneous communications between team members. Another important point Sunil raised was listening. We all need to feel we are listened to, but that can be difficult across distances and with different technologies. For the speaker to know others are paying attention, team members must ask questions, build on what was said, and help paraphrase and summarize.

'Let me see, what else was there. Ah yes, style. We feel it is important to put some personality into virtual communications so that you engage hearts as well as minds. Also, because we are all individuals, we think it's important everyone be able to participate in their own way. Some people like to write, some are good talkers, and others are good visually.

'What I can do, Will, is to write my notes up for you in a bit more detail. That should help with your Briefing Report.'

'Brilliant. Thanks. Perhaps all those reporting back could do the same. OK, let's go to cohesion and Zivah.'

'Thanks Will. We took a similar approach to Robert. Our first thinking was around team identity, not in terms of all having a team tee-shirt or logo (although we don't mind having a team name) but more around shared purpose and direction, and common norms and values for working together. These are important threads that help bind the team together. Alignment is critical, so communication opportunities need to be created to reinforce these threads.

'In our minds, one of the other key areas for building cohesion is documentation. We've all had bad experiences of never receiving a written plan of action or notes from virtual meetings. We have often been left to ourselves to fill in gaps, and a lot of the time it is pure guesswork. Whatever can be documented in terms of roles, processes, workflows, methods, and so on, helps the team feel it is acting together.

'The continuous sharing of information also helps; no matter where team members are located, if they all have access to key information, they will feel able to speak with one voice about the team and the project.

'That's a quick summary, Will. Like Robert, we'll get our notes to you asap.'

'Thanks Zivah. I'm getting the feeling that engagement, cohesion, and clarity are three sides of the same coin, if you get my meaning. OK Emily over to you.'

'Three sides of the same coin. Hang on Will, I'm having a zen moment … actually, we feel the same way. Transparency was key for us; making things as visible to the team as is possible – whether it is plans, decision making, feedback on team performance, or conflicts. Virtual team members already have restricted vision; they don't need additional blindfolds.

'Related to what I've just said is communicating the big picture. Virtual team members often have very partial views of the whole, and so periodically it is good to see things in context.

'What else? I can't read my own handwriting. Yes, open dialogue aimed at mutual understanding and learning. If team members are to be really clear about what is going on and why, they need to dig beneath the surface of information. They need to understand the assumptions and perspectives that drive different approaches. Very often, they need to understand the environment in which other team members are working so they can appreciate the challenges in different locations.

'We also feel it is important for the team to have protocols about the different forms of communication, for example e-mails and teleconferences. We're lucky because we have GO*dz*W*illa* to provide guidelines when we need them.'

As you can see, the result was a bit of a brain dump by everyone, but I was satisfied with the amount we had achieved in the time we had.

At the end of the session, I asked Aki if she would stay on to talk with me. I apologized and asked her to forgive my being a clown on our earlier call. I didn't think that was enough, however, so I explained how exactly I had played with language to give her a 'hard time'. I was absolutely not making fun of her English. She was confused as to why anyone would want to give someone else a 'hard time' unless you didn't like the person. 'It's difficult to explain,' I said, 'and it has to do with the English sense of humour, which I think is a mystery of the highest magnitude to the rest of the world.' She accepted my apology and said that she may have misinterpreted my intent. Although she said I was forgiven, I don't think relationships are so easily repaired. She will be guarded for a while when communicating with me, and I will be ultra cautious communicating with her. I think what I should have done was to have this conversation with video as well as audio. It would have been good to communicate with the face as well as with words.

After my conversation with Aki, I tried to reach the Diceman again, but still no answer. Was he still afloat?

ONE TECHNOLOGY DOESN'T FIT ALL

Got an e-mail this morning from Zivah in Tel Aviv. One topic we hadn't really discussed in the *Indaba* session, he said, was the use of technology. As Marshall McLuhan had said, 'The Medium is the Message', and so Zivah wanted to make sure that I make some reference in the report to how different technologies should be used in communication. He mentioned that he had once received some quite negative feedback from his manager via e-mail. He found that approach to be really demeaning, like he was a nonperson, an unfeeling robot (the medium being very much a part of the message). In his view, wasn't he – Zivah – worth at least a phone call in which the matter could be discussed human being-to-human being?

After looking for inspiration in *The Wit's End*, I thought about collaboration as being relatively Simple or Complex. In Simple Collaboration, issues are relatively well-defined, a significant portion of work is autonomous and routine, content is structured, static and to a large degree unambiguous, participants are small in number, and represented business functions are few. The opposites are true in Complex Collaborations. With collaborative technologies, we could think about them as being either Real-Time Interaction or Delayed-Time Interaction. After stealing more of Spinks' espresso beans, I drew this:

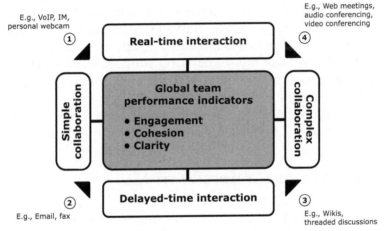

Match the right technology to the right job.

Each technological quadrant can contribute to global virtual team success in different ways.

Quadrant 1: Simple Collaboration – Real-Time Interaction

These technologies are good for helping solve relatively easy problems between small numbers of people. They are also good for starting and maintaining one-on-one relationships. Phone/VoIP is appropriate for giving personal feedback, while IM is not. Those technologies using voice rather than just text help convey personality and a higher degree of contextual information (e.g. feelings), although emotions can supplement text in instant messaging. One-on-one real-time interaction via a voice/webcam technology is best for handling low-level conflict. Ideally, higher-level conflict would be managed face-to-face.

Quadrant 2: Simple Collaboration – Delayed-Time Interaction

Technologies such as e-mail and fax are good for exchanges of factual information such as reports, instructions, and specifications, but not for taking decisions. Decision making is best done in a real-time setting. Information conveyed in e-mails and faxes can be specific and precise and this helps promote cohesion and clarity, but does little for engagement. When information is ambiguous or unstructured, or a deep, shared understanding needs to be developed, it is best to supplement these technologies with those enabling reflection, real-time dialogue, and group visualization.

Quadrant 3: Complex Collaboration – Delayed-Time Interaction

In more complex collaborations, technologies such as wikis and threaded discussions allow for reflection on a specific issue and the gathering of multiple viewpoints in one place. This can save the time often needed to consolidate the views expressed in multiple e-mails or minimize the 'dead gaps' in real-time brainstorming sessions. While such technologies may not promote the highest levels of engagement and cohesion, they can help make transparent the thinking of people on the team as well as help trigger creativity.

Quadrant 4: Complex Collaboration – Real Time Interaction

These technologies promote open dialogue and are particularly useful when issues are still ambiguous. Unless managed well they can be expensive in time expended. It is usually best to use them after some initial work has been done in Quadrant 2 or Quadrant 3 technologies, where some of the early thinking, structuring, clarifying, and sense making has already been done. This approach also facilitates input from those cultural groups who prefer to think responses through before sharing them.

TALKING LOUDER PROBABLY WON'T HELP

This morning, I went downstairs to talk to someone in Accounts about some expenses. Spinks was on the phone with Maintenance even though his desk is right next door to their room. It seems that his desk and chair have been superglued to the floor, at an unworkable distance from each other (it's not me, I swear to you). Maintenance will still try to avoid his calls, but it's harder for them to ignore him. When he gets through they will put him on hold for big chunks of time or pass him from one person to the next until he ends up with the young lad, Griff, who runs errands. Griff, a Scottish Nationalist from Glasgow, usually hasn't a clue what Spinks is talking about and Spinks can't understand a word Griff is saying. They think by shouting at each other eventually one of them will understand, or at least surrender. Speaking the same language doesn't mean that you're speaking the same language.

Nisha says she continues to make baby-step progress with Spinks. They have even had lunch together, although he seemed very nervous about running into any of his racist cronies on the street. Spinks, of course, doesn't see himself as a racist, but as a 'realist'. Nisha, as I've said before, believes in the powers of kindness and conversation. I don't know how she tolerates him being around her. I'm still not ready to meet with him and I know the multicultural Maintenance crew would like to boil him alive in his Earl Grey tea.

AND WHAT DID WE LEARN AT WORK TODAY?

Spent two hours on a conference call this morning and kept wondering why my comments were being ignored. What rude, ignorant (censored) I said to myself until I realized I'd been on mute the whole time!

CULTURAL INTELLIGENCE

THERE ARE CULTURES AND THERE ARE CULTURES

I remember a day when I was living in a ground floor flat in Clapham, South London. A young lad of about 12 threw half a brick through my front window. I chased him and caught him at the end of the street.

'What did you do that for you little wretch?' I shouted at him while grabbing on to the hood of his sweatshirt. He just shrugged his shoulders and said, 'Dunno.'

'Come on, why in hell's name did you smash my window you moronic little twerp?'

He looked me straight in the eyes and said without blinking, 'Whooligan culture. Tha's whot me probation officer cawls it. I jus' cawls it 'avin a laff.' I was so taken aback, I let him go with just a slap across the head.

'I could sue u fer tha',' he yelled while running away and giving me an obscene gesture.

So hooligans have their own culture, and that raised a troubling question in my mind. If I took the little devil to Court, would the judge say, 'I won't prosecute because breaking windows is part of his culture?' Hmmm. More seriously, I've read news reports of men who beat their wives near to death and are let off because its 'part of their culture'. Is this what multiculturalism means? Should we be thinking about it in a more sophisticated way? What if I knew a young woman was in danger of being the victim of a family honour killing? Would I warn her and find her shelter or shrug my shoulders and resign myself to those with 'cultural authority' over her? Putting a brick through my window and killing a young woman are obviously different in the extreme, but … that's enough thinking for today, and maybe tomorrow.

PARTY TIME

There's been a debate going on in *The Fun House* about what to call the … the end of the year party? Many want to keep calling it the Christmas Party because anything else would smack of American political correctness. Even the militant atheists have come out for Christmas party – apparently they are more anti-political correctness than they are anti-Christmas. Some want Holiday Party, but most find that too bland and once again too American. Some want New Year's party, but realize that might not be to the liking of many of our Asian colleagues who would not be celebrating New Year at that time. SHE has declared that Moonbeam will be organizing the party and so she will choose the name. We all wait with baited breath.

MEETING IN A SAFE PLACE

I knew that Ruth had attended some training sessions on culture and business to help with her international marketing efforts, so I e-mailed her to see if she would go out for a drink and a chat. She replied that given the traumatic experience we'd had with Paula at the last bar, perhaps it might be safer to meet via telephone. I could see from GO*dz*W*illa* that Ruth was working from home again so I called her there.

'Hi Ruth.'

The din at Ruth's end was deafening. I heard a youngster screech, 'Got the beasty by the tail.' I assumed the poor Rottweiler was taking another beating from the young Davian.

'Sorry Will, some of Davian's friends – more like fiends – are over. You'll have to speak up.'

'Ruth, I heard from SHE that you are interested in the culture stuff?' I said, trying to make myself heard.

'Right. Not sure I can tell you much, but I've got some good notes from the cross-cultural workshops I've sat in on.' I heard her yelling for Davian to stop the sword fight with Granny's knitting needles as she went off to find her notes.

'OK, I'm back. What would you like to know?'

'Let's start at the beginning and define culture.'

'OK. From my notes, culture is defined as the pattern of beliefs, values, assumptions, and attitudes that define the way of life of a group. The pattern is like a code, and when you can break the code much of what people do in the group and how they think starts to make sense. I'm going to e-mail you a phrase.'

Up on my screen, I saw: Thnmtsrrnngthsylm.

'What's this?' I asked.

'Let's assume the phrase is a culture. It's different from yours in two important respects.'

'There are no vowels, and if it's a phrase, there are no spaces between words.'

'Correct. Given that knowledge you should be able to decode the culture.'

It took me a while, but eventually I was able to understand the meaning: The inmates are running the asylum. 'That's the way I feel about my home life,' she said plaintively.

'So, how do you go about decoding a real culture?' I asked.

'There are different models of cultural difference that can be useful.'

At that moment, one of Davian's friends came to her to complain that Frederick was not letting him play on the bombsite in the living room. Ruth went off to make sure everyone was given equal access.

'What else is good to know?' I asked, when she returned.

'She talked about the iceberg model of culture. Parts of what make up a culture are on the surface of life – architecture, art, food and drink, body language and gestures, and rituals. The tricky stuff, she said, is below the water line: the values, beliefs, and assumptions that really drive behaviour in the group. These relatively hidden cultural preferences are the ones that can really trip us up; we need to be able to recognize them and understand their potential impact on us.'

'That's good to know. Anything else she said that might be useful?'

'Well ... she was very big on distinguishing between stereotypes and tendencies.'

'How?'

'She defined stereotypes as fixed images or associations we have about groups. Stereotypes don't leave room for individual variations. So, if you said to me that you are Swedish, I might have associations that, for me, describe *all* Swedes. And, if I say things like "Swedes are always like that, they always do it that way" then you can be sure I'm operating from a stereotype. I wouldn't be relating to *you* at all, but with an image of a group of which you are a member. You, of course, could belong to many groups.'

'And tendencies?'

'We know that groups have certain shared characteristics, but they are tendencies, not absolutes. Not everyone in the group will act or think in the same way. And we don't work with a culture, but with individuals who can sometimes have many cultural influences. Whatever I think I know about a culture must always be modifiable based on my real interactions with people from that group.'

'So, why do I need to know about culture at all if everyone is an individual?' I asked her.

'Because cultural tendencies do exist, and they do influence our behaviours and perceptions. If you know there is a tendency in Germany to speak very directly, you are less likely to take offence when you encounter that cultural style. You, personally, are not being singled out for direct talk.'

'It all sounds very complex.'

'It is. Cultures these days can be quite a cocktail mix. Cultural influences are flowing around the planet in a great swirl – in real life and on the Internet. This is one reason why it is so important to focus on the individual. Who knows what influences someone has grown up with?'

'Can you say anything about cultural intelligence, which is a term Sunil uses?'

'Hmmm, no. Can't help.'

Another friend of her dear son came to tell Ruth that Davian was taking sheets off her bed so that he could parachute from the top of the wardrobe. The friend didn't want to get blamed if things didn't work out well.

'Sorry, Will. I don't know how he thinks he's going to get to the top of the wardrobe, but I have no doubt he'll find a way. Bye for now.'

I couldn't help but think that one day Davian might become an icon in the so-called hooligan culture – either that or a Member of Parliament.

HOLY SPINKS!

I don't know how she does it, but Moonbeam has discovered the latest Spinks strategy for getting a love life – he's joining several evangelical churches! Why on earth, you might be asking? Apparently, there's new research from America showing that evangelical teens, at least in the States, are more promiscuous than those from other religious groups.[23] He does put a lot of faith in American research, given his fear that all things British are becoming Americanized. Still, I suppose he sees some advantage in believing the research, so will adopt it wholeheartedly. Cognitive dissonance is everyone's friend.

---

[23] Spinks got his information while browsing on the Web. It was in an article by Hannah Rosin called 'Even Evangelical Teens Do It', *Slate Magazine*, 30 May 2007. The article was based on the work of Dr Mark Regnerus and published in *Forbidden Fruit: Sex and Religion in the Lives of American Teenagers* (Oxford University Press, 2007).

THE EXTENDED NETWORK

This morning I e-mailed Sunil asking if he could point me in the direction of someone who could talk to me about cultural intelligence. I received a reply that I should speak with a good friend of his in the US, Truman Beardsley, who is now a high-flying global management consultant. Sunil will let him know I'll be getting in touch.

WHO REALLY WANTS TO BE IN THE REAL WORLD ANYMORE?

Gary Botchnik, one of my former classmates in the New York MBA programme, called me this morning to tell me he was coming over to London (his first trip to the UK) and he would love to meet up.

He asked me a few questions about England, but soon the conversation turned to talking about our most embarrassing moments during our travels. I told him of the time I was staying in a hotel at Narita Airport, outside of Tokyo. After travelling for many hours, and before going to bed, I felt the deep desire to take a swim. Down to the pool area I went and tried to communicate to the lovely Japanese lady handing out towels that I needed to borrow something to swim in. It was tough going until I said 'Speedo' – ah, the power of brands. Off she went and returned with a box full of bathing suits. She looked at me closely and then rummaged through the box. After a minute of shaking her head and making incomprehensible sounds, she pulled out a suit and gave it to me. She couldn't help but giggle – politely, behind her hand – as she turned and headed into the women's changing room.

The 'Speedo' turned out to be a Japanese extra large, but would barely fit over one of my thighs. Although it took me the best part of 10 minutes – and a lot of dancing on one leg around the changing room – I managed to pull, tug, jerk, wrench, and lever the Speedo over both thighs and up to my middle. Even when it reached my middle, it didn't really pack everything in. It was one of those times when you've gone so far with a project that turning back is the worst option you can imagine – no one wants to cut his or her losses and get out. Actually, I wasn't sure if I could get out of this particular project.

No matter how much I pushed and probed, I couldn't insert all the necessary bits and pieces of my anatomy into the swimsuit. Having come this far, however, I was determined to accomplish my goal of taking a swim. I picked up my tiny towel, tried to cover as much of my middle as I could, then walked painfully past the women's dressing room to the pool. I say 'walked', but I had very restricted motion. I was moving like a desperately-needing-to-pee-zombie leaving a ballet lesson – high on tiptoes, knees locked, and with each step being more of a lunging swivel of the hip and a dead foot flopping forward. A few ladies came out of their dressing room, but quickly ducked back inside when they saw this strange foreigner in contortions in the corridor. I made it to the pool, but the space between where you left your sandals and towel and the water was about 10 metres. There were several Japanese couples already in the water, but I speculated that if I was quick enough they wouldn't see me jump in. I waddled as quickly as I could to the pool's edge and jumped. Unfortunately, the water at this end of the pool was only about 45 centimetres deep and the impact of my hitting the bottom split the Speedo at the seams and sent it hurtling towards the nearby Japanese couples. They were sitting on the bottom of the pool, not standing up as I had assumed. I yelped and ducked down into the water as far as nature and the water would allow me. The Japanese sat with their mouths gaping; eventually, one of them stood up and returned my shredded Speedo to me. He was very gracious, I have to say. It was then I heard the applause. On a balcony up to my left was part of the hotel gym. A group of Americans who had been beating treadmills to a pulp had stopped to watch my scintillating performance. At this point, I resigned myself to the fates. I stood up, waved, bowed, and left the pool clutching my disintegrated Speedo to what was left of my manhood.

The Japanese hotel staff were very polite, but asked me please not to 'express myself' in the pool again during my stay. I said that I had not been trying to express myself in the pool, but they said I had whether I had meant to or not. I stayed in my room and ordered room service for the rest of my trip.

What had I learned? While working virtually across geographies and cultures has its drawbacks, it's often much kinder to the ego and one's personal sense of dignity.

RISKY BUSINESS

I got Truman Beardsley on the phone this afternoon. He said he didn't have a lot of time, but he would help if he could. Sunil had filled him in on the new workplace project, so we leapt straight into the subject.

'Sunil says you are interested in the idea of cultural intelligence,' I said.

'That's right. I've been studying cross-cultural management for some years. First, let me say what I mean by cultural intelligence. Despite globalization, there are still pronounced cultural differences in the world, even in the workplace, and I see cultural intelligence as the ability to "read" and understand different ways of being-in-the-world and to apply that understanding to achieving goals.'

'It sounds somewhat manipulative,' I said.

'Oh, it can be,' Truman added quickly, 'if it is simply self-serving. If you are trying to find ways to work effectively with others, to communicate better and promote mutual interests, then I think it can be beneficial to everyone. I do a lot of work with young men and women in India who are working for US or European businesses. They understand they are working for companies whose cultural milieu is very distant from their own. Their primary objective is to learn how to succeed in that different cultural environment.'

'How do you help them?'

'A while back, I developed a framework to help me be more intelligent across a range of cultures. I was doing a lot of travelling at the time and couldn't keep up with learning about every culture I was visiting. You see, years ago being culturally intelligent was about learning some do's and taboos before travelling. There's still some value in that if you know specifically what culture you are going to be interacting with, but I see that approach as being narrowly knowledge-focused rather than broadly intelligence-focused. If I'm culturally intelligent, I should be able to go into any culture and understand and adapt relatively quickly.'

'That's good. I like that approach. But how do you do it?'

'I developed what I call the RISK™ framework for cultural intelligence.'

'I hope this is the last acronym I have to absorb for years to come,' I said.

'Ha ha, I doubt that, Will. Money and acronyms make the world go around. In applying cultural intelligence, the first thing you need to do is to be able to recognize what cultural differences are bumping up against one another. So, the R in RISK is for Recognize. To help me recognize cultural differences, I developed a model I call the Worldprism™.'

'Worldprison?'

'Worldprism™, Will. When we look at the world around us, we take for granted that we see the world as it really is, but of course we don't. We see it through our own cultural lens. We might see the same object or behaviour, but it can mean totally different things to us. In your culture you might see a plain old rock to pick up and skim across the river, while in my culture I see a sacred stone that must not be touched. I'll e-mail you the model.'

'Thanks. What about the rest of RISK™?'

'Sure. The "I" stands for Impact. Once you've identified differences, you need to think about the potential impact they could have on working together. Let's say, for example, that you are very Task-focused while I am Relationship-focused. In my culture, things get done when a relationship is in place. I know you and trust you so I will do whatever I can to meet your needs. You, on the other hand, are less concerned about whether or not we have a relationship. You have a good plan with targets and milestones, and you put your faith in the plan. So business for you is relatively impersonal.

'This difference can impact many things, like the importance you and I put in written agreements, how we go about hiring people, or even how we approach sales and marketing.'

'I see. That's very interesting,' I said. 'So, in terms of hiring people, for example, you are more likely to hire people you know or are known to others you trust. You are also more likely to do business with a handshake, while I must have a detailed, signed, and sealed contract.'

'That's right. You've got it. The "S" in RISK is for Strategy. How are you going to manage the differences to achieve the best outcome? There are several options. First, you can adapt by adjusting your style. Let's say I'm from an individualistic culture and you are from a more group-oriented culture. In my individualistic culture, I probably give you direct feedback in a one-on-one meeting. I would discuss your strengths with you as well as areas where you needed to improve. In more group-oriented cultures like those in Asia, the feedback would be much more indirect. I might not even speak to you one-on-one for fear of you losing face. I might speak to the whole team instead.'

I thought about that for a moment. 'Not sure I'd get the message,' I said.

'Right, but you are used to a very different and more direct communication style. You don't know what subtle signals to look for.'

'That's true. You said adapting was just one option.'

'Yes, you can also blend differences to create something of a hybrid that, given the context, draws on the best of the different approaches. Another option is what I call cultural co-creation, where instead of a focus on your culture and my culture we focus on *our* culture, our team culture.'

'So, you work with teams to define their shared cultural norms and practices?'

'Correct. Now there may be situations where you just let people do their own thing. The fact that we do things differently might not impact our working together at all. So we leave each other alone. There may also be situations, of course, when someone needs to enforce an approach. There could be a company policy that says that no matter where you are in the world, *this* approach must be followed, it is non-negotiable.'

'Like our company code of conduct.'

'Absolutely. The "K" stands for Know-how. All the good work done so far in recognizing differences, understanding their impact, and strategizing the best way forward may come to nothing if we don't have the know-how to manage ourselves. You need to control potentially destructive feelings, thoughts, and behaviours so you can build bridges across the cultural gaps, not widen them.'

'Can you give me some examples?'

'Impatience is one that needs to be controlled. Even when you are working virtually it is easy to communicate your impatience and frustration. On the phone, you might interrupt more, blow air through your teeth, sigh, rush to close off discussions, or stop participating. Even in instant messaging you can sense if you are losing someone. Typed messages might become more abrupt, or emoticons might disappear from the text.

'In terms of thinking, stereotyping is obviously something you need to control. Minimizing differences also needs to be controlled. I remember my wife making her first trip to Japan. I offered her some tips about Japanese culture, but she declined. I'll just be myself, she said, and I'm sure we'll all get along. The day after she arrived, I received a message on my PDA, *HELP ME! TIPS NOW!*'

'And behaviour?'

'Obvious things like body language and gestures, but I think the real damaging behaviours are more subtle. Talking too much before listening and not observing is one. Demonstrating disinterest in others is another. People want respect, and listening and getting to know them and their culture are important. I'll email you some more for your briefing report.'

'That's great. Many thanks Truman, and have a good ... Chris ... holiday,' I stuttered, catching myself before making a potentially politically incorrect *faux pas*. I didn't know what faith or no-faith Truman might be.

'You have a good Chrisholiday too, Will.'

WE WISH YOU A MERRY ...

This morning, Moonbeam released the name of her end of the year party. She said that her first thought was to give the party an actual person's name like Charlie, Louise, or Vladimir [or Chris, I thought], but then she decided people names were too rooted in different cultures. She then thought about having just a number depending on what evening of the week it was; e.g. Friday would be number 6. It could also be the actual date, of course, but then how would she write it? December 6th, 2008 could be 6/12/08 or 12/6/08 or even 2008/12/6. She could just use 2008, but for some groups that wouldn't be correct. Numbers, it seemed to her, also had too many cultural biases. She then thought about having a random series of symbols, but she thought even this was risky given the potency of symbols in different cultures.

Even though she realized it was created out of English letters, what she did was to call the party by a meaningless acronym that people could read into whatever they wanted – whether they were Atheist, Christian, Hindu, Jewish, Muslim, Pagan or whatever (like me). She created the acronym by closing her eyes and banging on her keyboard twice with her right elbow: LLONNYJ is what came out. Some have already complained that the double LLs at the beginning make it appear too biased towards the Welsh. Others have raised the possibility of a calculated pro-American slant given the (so-called 'random' – yeah, right!) inclusion of NY. Some want to know if the 'J' after 'NY' refers to Jews, and couldn't that be considered pro-Israel or perhaps anti-Semitic? One person from HR wanted to know if the 'O' was symbolic of peoples and cultures coming together at the party in a har-monious whole, in which case she was all for it. Moonbeam nearly lost her cool on several occasions. 'I just banged my right elbow on the stupid keyboard a couple of times!' she would yell at people who seemed on the verge of asking her a question. The conspiracy theorists among us have been doing Google searches for L. Lonny J just in case there is a subliminal advertisement in there for a friend of our party coordinator. Some are really getting into it and have signs on their desks saying, C U @ LLONNY Js! Human beings – we're a weird lot.

DOMESTIC BLISS

If you remember, Sadie and Daniel had invited me to their house for dinner. Tonight was the night for experiencing their domestic bliss first hand. They live in West London, near Richmond, not far from where the Diceman had had his houseboat moored on the River Thames (yes, it had failed to rise with the tide and he was now sleeping in *The Fun House* until substantial repairs could be made to the rotted hull). Before the journey out there, I looked up 'Domestic Bliss' on Wikipedia only to find there wasn't an entry. Interesting!

I have to confess, I was dreading the dinner (neither Daniel nor Sadie could cook very well), and because Alice couldn't be there (remember Alice who Sadie wanted to fix me up with) I was most likely going to have to endure my ex-best friend and ex-girlfriend telling me in the most loving and caring terms how they never meant to hurt me – it just happened.

Actually, the evening went off rather well – at least from my point of view. Food had been ordered from the local Indian restaurant, and Sadie and Daniel spent the time clawing at each other like angry ferrets. It was wonderful entertainment. We all drank too much wine, and the more we drank, the louder and more vicious Daniel and Sadie became. All I had to do was sit back, eat, drink, and be merry while my two ex-friends scratched, bit, and tore at each other. Great fun.

When I'd had my fill, I got up to leave. Sadie hugged me and the old feelings of love and longing ripped through me like a shock wave. Daniel staggered with me to the door and we both stepped out into the damp, foggy night. I told him to go back inside, but instead he clung to me and spilled out a confession.

'Will ... I'm such a damn fool ... I shouldn't have married Sadie,' he slobbered. 'I ... I ... I've met someone else.'

'You've what?' I screamed back at him.

'Shush ... I know ... it's ... it's not right, but I can't help it. I'm ... I'm madly in love with her.'

'Who? You idiot. How did this happen?'

'The Internet. Second Life.'

'What! You have actually met this woman face-to-face haven't you?' I said, believing Daniel was crazy enough to fall in love with a gorgeous avatar that would turn out to be a flesh and blood Sumo wrestler from Kyoto.

'Oh yes. We've been seeing each other ... a few times ... it's amazing ... us ... together.'

'I don't believe this,' I said angrily. 'You marry my girl-friend, and then you want to dump her after a couple of years for someone you hardly know.'

'I know ... it sounds crazy ... but Paula's different.'

'Paula?'

'Yeah, that's her name. She's a journalist. So beautiful, so smart. She's just had her heart broken by some jerk. She found him in a Wine Bar with another woman.'

I was speechless and struggling to take it all in. Paula and Daniel. It can't be, surely. Are the fates smiling down on me at last? 'What are you going to do?' I asked quietly.

'I have to be with Paula. You're my friend. What do you think?'

What do I think? Daniel was obviously *the* man … the one I wasn't half of according to Paula. I thought about Sadie being a free agent, and the foulest devil in me made me say, 'Well Dan, follow your bliss as they say. Go get her tiger!' As soon as the words left my mouth I felt wracked with guilt, but not enough to put things straight.

Waiting for the train home, I mumbled a prayer to the Internet. 'Oh blessed electronic god divine, I am your most humble and faithful servant. I pledge my deep adoration to you always; may you forever bring my foes together where they can torture each other and leave me free and in peace.'

When the train rolled in a kindly old lady took me by the arm and guided me through the carriage doors. 'You should be at home dear,' she whispered in my ear, 'with a nice cup of warm milk, a bit of whisky in it, and a few aspirins. That'll put you right.'

BUYING TIME

Sadie sent me an IM this morning:

Sadie: Will, I'm desperate. What am I going to do? Daniel's left me for a weirdo journalist he met on the Internet. He finds her different and exciting! Help me.

I felt in the iron jaws of an impossible dilemma. What do I say? If I say 'I know,' she'll say, 'I thought you were my friend. Why didn't you tell me?' If I lie and act totally stunned – and if by chance we were to pair up again in the future – she might find me out as a liar and that could be a disaster. What if she found out I didn't try to dissuade Daniel, but actually went some way to encouraging him, what then? I messaged back.

Will: Meet for lunch at *The Devil's Stewpot*.

At least that gave me a little time.

I WANTED TO TELL ALL, I REALLY DID

During my ride in to work this morning, I listened to a podcast about the Internet revolution – how it is enabling everyone to live out their fantasy lives. Not sure I have a fantasy life. Sad isn't it!

While I waited for Sadie in the restaurant, I pondered on whether the Internet has a culture of its own – that was a question raised in the podcast. Many times, I think it's a mutation of the hooligan culture. I've read bits and pieces referring to it as libertarian, anarchic, democratic, participatory, narcissistic, or even a severe case of electronic flatulence. I suppose it's all of those things, and more. Looking out of the *Stewpot* window at the bent figures stooped under umbrellas, I thought of the Internet as a vast, unplanned, sprawling city like London. The mind-numbingly stupid are there, as well as the brilliantly-brilliant and super-creative. Parts are trashy, crass, and vulgar, while other parts are classy and sophisticated. It's a whirl and buzz of activity, some of it meaningful, but lots just pointless and not even entertaining. Some parts might actually be dangerous. London is so fascinating because it contains such a mess of rich and juicy flavours. In its own way the city is a stewpot full of different ingredients, some of which you can leave in the pot or on the side of your plate. You choose. And the Internet is its own human stewpot, although some might call it the devil's stewpot! I'm rambling like a lost sheep, which is what my sister says I am.

Lunch with Sadie was 'interesting' as we say in Britain. I had decided to tell her the truth about knowing the Daniel–

Paula situation, but with Sadie crying in my arms in the restaurant, I couldn't think how I was going to explain. Between mournful cries she gasped, 'Why? Oh Will, why didn't *we* stay together?'

'You dumped me for Daniel,' I said trying to stifle any hint of bitterness.

'Oh right.'

At that moment Sadie's phone beeped. It was a text message from the double dealer himself. *Sadie, have made a huge mistake. Must see you. 10 minutes at our special place. How much I love you. Danny.* Sadie leapt up spilling hot goulash. Off she went babbling apologies and thanking me for being such a good listener and friend. I wonder what happened to change Daniel's mind about Paula? Couldn't wait to hear that story.

Then, a ghastly thought made me tremble. What if Daniel had mentioned to Paula that his best friend was called Will Williams? What if Paula assumed I had been the cause of Daniel breaking up with her? (Censored).

My phone beeped. It was a text from Sophie: 'Miss u lots.' [Heavy sigh. Beat myself on head with phone.] I have absolutely no doubt that Sophie is a truly special person in my life. She really is. I adore her. So what madness makes me cling hopelessly to the Sadie shipwreck? As Sophie says to me often, 'Oh what fools we mortals be.'

WHERE THE ACTION IS

'An interesting clash of cultures,' said Sunil.

I was on another conference call with Sunil in India, Robert and Emily in the US, and Anton in Germany. Sunil had been talking for some time about continuing to leverage outsourcing opportunities in India. Robert was getting impatient. I could tell by the way he was breathing – a lot of exhaling that was quite loud and prolonged.

'What do you mean an interesting clash of cultures?' Emily asked Sunil.

'Robert is losing patience with me, I can tell,' said Sunil without any bad feeling.

'No, no,' replied Robert. 'Well, maybe I am.'

'I think it is fairly well known that America tends to be an action-oriented culture,' Sunil continued. 'In fact, when I was a consultant in the US, someone said to me, "Sunil, get to the point quicker. Remember that we Americans are human doings rather than human beings."'

'You're right, Sunil. I'm a doer,' said Robert, laughing. 'We tend not to be very patient. Speed wins. That's our theory and we're sticking to it.'

'That's absolutely fine in some circumstances,' said Sunil, 'but I come from a culture that tends to focus on the reasoning process. Robert, you want to know what to do and I want to know how to think about something. Both approaches can add value.'

'That's cool Sunil. I can relate to that,' said Emily, obviously wowed by Sunil's insight. 'After leaving college, I travelled through India. *We* do approach and talk about problems differently. I hadn't really thought about it before.'

'Yeah, thanks Sunil. A little self-awareness never hurt anyone,' said Robert. 'We should probably have these culture chats more often.'

'I agree,' replied Sunil, with laughter in his voice. 'I think it's very useful for global teams like ours to openly explore our differences. There is value in all cultural orientations, as well as potential drawbacks to them. What is best depends on the context. Ideally, we would all recognize the value of our differences and be able to flex between them depending on what we are trying to accomplish.'

'Ideally, we should see ourselves as complementing one another,' said Robert. 'I just wanted you to be more like me.'

Sunil laughed and said that he would try to become more of an 'action man', but couldn't guarantee a complete transformation. 'Important for our working together,' Sunil said, 'are certain basic conditions. Mutual respect and openness are critical. Without them people don't listen to one another and no real dialogue takes place. Without dialogue there is no learning and without learning there is no mutual understanding. I fear listening is a dying art. All we want to do these days is take a fixed position and beat people over the head with it; that might attract ratings for so-called chat shows, but it doesn't advance humanity very far.'

'I see your point,' said Robert. 'Let's do some more thinking and then we'll decide on a course of action.'

I asked if we could quickly move on because I had something I needed to do. If the others could have thrown things at me they would have – another good reason to work virtually.

FATE SMILES ON CRABTREE

Moonbeam came in all smiles this morning. 'You look like a cat who has just had her litter changed,' I said.

'Godmother Isis is working her magic for me, Will.'

'Really? It's helpful to have a personal relationship with a deity.'

'Poor Arthur had a kickboxing tournament last night and he's broken his right leg. You can go and see it happening on *YouTube*. Ironic isn't it. Arthur is the one who's on a video for the world to see; it's already had 2000 hits. He's a star and enjoying every minute of it. It's really horrible seeing his leg flopping about like a boiled celery stick, but he's happy. Let me show you.'

A tiny voice inside me said *you are what you Google*, so I declined. Sensitive lad that I am, I'd also eaten some leftover sushi for breakfast and was reluctant to part with it so soon.

'Moonbeam, have you no compassion?' I asked.

'I did for a while in the hospital, but as soon as I saw the gluttonous way he scoffed down his instant celebrity, I thought I'd become ill. He's already had three marriage proposals. The last thing on his mind right now is the Crabtree video.'

She kissed her Isis pendant and skipped over to her desk humming *Celebration* by Kool and the Gang. I only know the song because it used to be one of my father's favourites. *Note to self: I must contact my Dad and see how he's doing.*

SEEING THE WORLD THROUGH A CULTURAL LENS

I received an e-mail from Truman Beardsley with his World-prism™ model of culture. The differences in the model were divided into three dimensions – Relating: how we typically interact with one another; Regulating: how we typically manage the world around us; Reasoning: how we typically think about and explain things.

I think it makes more sense for me to show you rather than tell you:

Dimensions	Cultural differences
Relating	Task–Relationship Focus
	Explicit–Implicit Communication
	Individual–Group Identity
Regulating	Risk-Taking–Risk-Avoiding Preference
	Tight–Loose Use of Time
	Shared–Concentrated Power
Reasoning	Linear–Circular Processing
	Facts–Thinking Emphasis
	Simple–Complex Explanations

I managed to contact him on his mobile phone. He was in his hotel room in Lagos, Nigeria. 'Thanks very much for the model, Truman.'

'Any part that seems unclear to you?' he asked.

'I've come across most of these differences, some quite recently. I suppose you give people a questionnaire to help identify which cultural orientations they tend to favour.'

'Right. It helps build self-awareness.'

'If you don't mind me asking, which cultural orientations would best describe you?'

'Hang on and I'll e-mail you my profile. … As you can see, my dominant cultural positions tend to be down the left side, and many Americans will be similar. That said, however, my specific life experiences have had an impact.'

'In what way?'

'I grew up in quite an extended family and so my own profile shows less individualism than many Americans. I'm also less of a risk-taker than many. In my family caution was almost a sacred word.'

'What about linear and circular?'

'Oh, I'm pretty linear like most Americans. I like to go from A to B to C. I have to adapt to a more circular style when I'm in Nigeria. Discussions tend not to be step-by-step here; the tendency is to circle a topic looking at it from different points of view, and reaching a conclusion can be a lengthy process. But you can't force people down a linear path; you can only guide them back gently to what you see as your main topic and flow.'

RELATING	How we interact											
TASK	O	O	O	●	O	▬	O	O	O	O	O	RELATIONSHIP
EXPLICIT	O	O	O	O	●	▬	O	O	O	O	O	IMPLICIT
INDIVIDUAL	O	O	O	O	O	▬	●	O	O	O	O	GROUP
REGULATING	How we manage											
RISK TAKING	O	O	O	O	●	▬	O	O	O	O	O	RISK AVOIDING
TIGHT	O	O	O	●	O	▬	O	O	O	O	O	LOOSE
SHARED	O	O	●	O	O	▬	O	O	O	O	O	CONCENTRATED
REASONING	How we think											
LINEAR	O	O	●	O	O	▬	O	O	O	O	O	CIRCULAR
FACTS	O	O	O	●	O	▬	O	O	O	O	O	THINKING
SIMPLE	O	O	●	O	O	▬	O	O	O	O	O	COMPLEX

Truman Beardsley's Worldprism™ profile.

'Where do you think I would fit on your model?'

'Ha ha. You tell me, Will.'

'Interesting. Before I left to do my MBA in the US, my profile would have been different to what it is today. I think my experiences over there have shifted me more toward the left side, but not in every case. I was, and still am, more on the relationship side than most of my American colleagues. I think I've become more explicit in my communication, but having been back here for a while, I'm moving into being more implicit. Like you, I don't see myself as being far over on the individualist side, although others might see me differently. My risk-taking has increased since being in the States, and I can relate to a tight approach to time and a preference for shared power. I'm somewhat linear in my approach, although I think that tends to be forced upon me by my job rather than being my preferred style. I relate more to the thinking than the fact-driven side and, again, I think I've been forced by my job to adopt the simple approach to presenting issues. I see this could be useful on teams. Do team members typically share and discuss their profiles with each other?'

'Yes. When they've identified and shared their differences, they can go on to discuss their potential impact on activities like information sharing, making decisions, planning, communicating, and organizing. After that, they can work together to shape their shared team culture.'

'That's useful. Thanks Truman. So, have you been consulting in Nigeria for a while? I hear it's totally corrupt.'

'No, visiting family.'

'Oh, oh, I'm sorry ... I didn't mean to say. ...'

'It's OK, Will. Nigeria does have problems with corruption, as do many others.'

'I didn't realize. ...'

'That I'm what we call African-American.'

'No ... well. Yes, I suppose that's what I'm saying, maybe.'

'How would you know? We've only talked on the phone. Will you relate to me differently now?'

'No, no, no.'

'Will you think less of my ideas?'

'Absolutely not.'

'Will you. ...'

The conversation went on for a while. In my mind, I hadn't pictured Truman as African-American. Something in my voice must have alerted him to the fact that my mental image of who he was had suddenly spun 180 degrees. I have to confess, I had associated 'high flying global business consultant' with him being white – a truly racist assumption on my part. Be honest, before you read about his visiting family in Nigeria, how many of you assumed Truman was a white Caucasian male?

I thought back to what Truman had told me about self-management in our first conversation. Managing our thinking was one of the key areas. Based on my own life experiences, I had made some very wrong assumptions. Hopefully a lesson learned.

NOTHING MUCH TO CELEBRATE ON THE HOME FRONT

'Hello Darling.'

'Hello Mother. How is Dad doing?'

'And I suppose how I'm doing is of no consequence.'

'Well, yes of course.'

'The show is doing wonderfully. The reviews in the local press have been raving.'

She went on to tell me about the selfishness of others involved in the production and how they just wanted to hog the limelight. Prima donnas the lot of them.

'And how's Dad?'

'I don't know. You talk to him and see if you can get any sense.'

I feared he would come on the phone and be unable to communicate in any rational way, but he seemed well.

'They tell me I've got something called multi-infarct dementia,' he said cheerfully.

'Dementia! Oh my God. Dad.'

'Don't worry. I could live for years, although my mind might get a bit more wishy-washy as time goes by. It means I've had a few "silent strokes" and they can cause confusion and wandering. They can't do anything about brain damage already done, but they can try and prevent future strokes through managing my blood pressure and cholesterol. I'll be OK. Don't you worry.'

'I wish I lived closer, Dad.'

'No, no. I'll muddle through. You've got your own life to live. Everyone's mobile these days.'

'Why don't you let me set you up with a computer so that we can e-mail and chat?'

'You'd be wasting good money. Can't teach old dogs new tricks.'

'Love you, Dad.'

'Love you too, Will. Be good.'

LLONNYJs

Moonbeam had set the party up in a recording studio, which I thought was a brilliant idea. As well as overindulging in the usual food and drink, and being a complete fool on the dance floor, anyone so inclined could be recorded singing their favourite tune. Backing tracks were available for many songs – just like karaoke really – except that you walked away with the evidence on CD of how bad you were. Sophie was with me and we made a recording of the Beatles *Hey Jude*, with everyone joining in at the end to scream the la la la lalalala chant. It was really truly awful, but a potential collector's item, I'd say.

Sophie met Sadie and nothing happened. Everyone was very sociable. Sadie and Daniel were too absorbed in their rekindled love to pay us any real attention. Sophie asked me once if I wanted to leave because I kept looking at the door. I was just terrified that Paula would crash in and start a major riot.

In one area of the studio, Ruth's husband's band, *Lick Knuckle and the Resisting Fruit*, were playing their expanded repertoire of six songs. They made a demo tape of their punk version of the hymn Jerusalem. Another collector's item.

SHE was there by herself, which was disappointing because I was hoping to meet her partner and get the gay thing out in the open. I felt it was an unnecessary wall between us. Moonbeam was also by herself. Arthur was still recuperating from his kickboxing accident. I noticed Moonbeam and the Bugster getting cozy behind a kit of drums in a dark corner.

Nisha was there looking stunning in a red and gold sari. She asked me if I'd seen Spinks.

'You're asking the wrong person,' I said. 'If he doesn't show up that's fine with me.'

'Never give up, Will. He told me he would come tonight and apologize to you. Going to these Evangelical meetings seems to have done him some good. At one, a young woman started speaking in tongues, and he said he could understand everything. She seemed to be speaking directly to him, he said. From somewhere, he found the courage to invite her here tonight.'

Spinks never showed up, and come to think of it neither did anyone from Maintenance. Paula thankfully never burst through the doors to cause a scene; I hope and pray to *whoever or whatever* that that deranged episode in my life is finally over.

We all spilled on to the street at about 2 am clutching our pitiful CDs. Actually, that isn't entirely true because Moonbeam and the Bugster were locked in the studio all night.

FRANCE CALLING

The day after LLONNYJs SHE called me at 7 am.

'Sorry to call you so early Will.'

'It's OK. I have jet lag these days without ever leaving the country.'

'Would you like a short trip to foreign parts?'

'What do you mean?' Images of a gaming conference in Hawaii leapt into my head.

'I've had a call that the French authorities are holding Spinks.'

'What!'

'He was found relatively unconscious last night on a Channel ferry that landed in Calais. He was naked except for a pair of underpants emblazoned with the Union Jack and he'd been covered in black shoe polish.'

'Good God. How on earth did that happen?'

'He says he was kidnapped, got drunk, and the rest is a blank.'

'Who would do that?' As soon as the words left my mouth, I thought of the chaps in Maintenance who were not Spinks-friendly. None had shown up at the party.

'He didn't recognize any of them because their faces were covered by ski masks. Another thing they did was to scrawl "Traitor" across his chest.'

Why would the Maintenance crew do that? I wondered. 'Does Spinks have any theories?'

'You probably know he's been going to some Evangelical churches around London.'

'Yes'.

'Apparently he's fallen head over heels for a young woman in one of them who happens to be black.'

'Spinks!'

'Love is a potent force, Will. By the way, he thinks he recognized voices of some of his Anglo-Saxon Alliance friends.'

'What would you like me to do?'

'Go to his neighbour who has a key to his flat, find his passport, pick up some clothes, and convince the French authorities that Spinks is who he says he is. I'm leaving today for a gaming conference in Hawaii.'

'You could take me with you to carry your bags,' I pleaded.

'Sorry, Will. I have a friend already coming with me. Maybe next time.'

A mystery friend. I hate mysteries. 'Mind if I take Nisha with me?'

'Great idea. I know there's bad blood between you and Spinks, but right now even you should be a friendly face.'

'Don't worry. Spinks might be at a turning point. When the student is ready, the teacher will arrive.'

'That's Taoist isn't it? You going New Age on me, Will?' SHE said.

THE CROSSING

Crossing the Channel with Nisha was an opportunity to talk about her views on cultural intelligence. The ferry was tipping violently in a heavy swell and both of us were trying to keep our minds on something other than the boat's motion. We sat and shivered on deck where we could breathe the cold air and have quick access to the railing in case we needed to … you know. I explained to her what I'd learned so far.

'You got any advice on working across cultures?' I asked her as she clung white-knuckled to the bench we were sitting on.

'Has any one talked to you about self-management?' she shouted through the wind.

'Yes, Truman Beardsley, a consultant in the States talked about the importance of managing potentially destructive feelings, thoughts, and behaviours.'

'Good. That's so important. Let's be honest, working across cultures can be tough, even with the best will in the world. We get our buttons pushed – know what I mean.'

'I do. Things happen to cause us to lose our temper or get very impatient.'

'That's right. Can I tell you a process I learned?'

'Please do,' I answered, trying to find any horizon through the mist that I could stare at and pretend I was sitting still. 'Just don't give me another acronym to remember or I'll throw you overboard.'

'Well, you could make an acronym out of it if you wanted to.'

'I really don't.'

'OK. The first thing is to prepare. Research the likely differences you will encounter. By avoiding surprises, you can adjust more easily. Preparation helps set realistic expectations – don't assume that you or anyone else can get things done at the same speed as before. You'll be out of your comfort zone, sometimes feeling disorientated and off-balance – a bit like now really.'

'You can say that again,' I shouted back. My stomach was pin-balling between my head, my abdomen, and my feet.

'Next, you need to act on your current knowledge and understanding of the expected differences while listening and observing for them in real-time. Look out for hidden differences even though the surface may appear smooth. What you've told me about Truman Beardsley's model is a good way to begin getting at some of the differences beneath the surface.'

'A smooth surface would be nice,' I said woefully.

The wind was getting even stronger and Nisha had to speak directly into my ear with her hands acting like a megaphone. 'As you start working on a team, you need to check your responses as well as those of others. Are you staying calm, patient, and in control of yourself? How are others responding to you? Do they look or sound confused or upset? Apologize if you feel it is appropriate. Apologies can be very powerful.'

'Spinks had better apologize for putting us through this hell, as well as all the other (censored),' I groaned. The sea gulls seemed to be mocking our misery, as they swirled and cackled overhead. I cursed the disaster known as Spinks.

'Shall, I go on Will? You're turning a strange colour.' I nodded which was a mistake because my stomach lurched from my throat to my head and back to my throat. Luckily it stayed put and didn't try to escape. 'Finally, you need to apply what you've been learning in real-time. Keep on checking your own and others' reactions, and make adjustments as you need to.' I nodded again, but more gently.

'In a nutshell, the process is Prepare, Act, Check, Apply, or PACA for short.'

'That was an acronym, I thought you were my friend.'

With no warning, Nisha leapt from the bench and dashed to the railing. Poor Nisha sacrificed her breakfast to the sea. 'That was a surprise,' she moaned, lifting her head towards me. I had some tissues in my pocket so I gave them to her. Someone on the deck below was not at all happy. Suddenly my sickness was gone as I helped the shocked Nisha back to the bench. 'One last thing,' she said, 'for working across cultures and living life in general: always expect the unexpected!'

SHOWTIME:
ALL TOGETHER NOW!

SHE and I arrived at the TV studios two hours before the interview was to be recorded. Midge, a no-nonsense production assistant with serious looking headphones and clipboard took us to the set. Leaving us there, she went off to the control room for a pre-prod-conf as she called it, and told us to look around. 'Jus' don' touch anyfink. It's awl 'eld togever wiv tape an' pins,' were her ominous parting words.

There was a small raised platform on which a round table and two red leather chairs were placed. There were blue and white mugs on the table that I supposed were meant to give the set an air of informality. The backdrop was a large plywood wall on the front of which were blown-up photographs of the London, New York, Shanghai, and Tokyo skylines. On top of the photos were the show's logo and programme title: Inside Trends – Revolution in the Workplace. There were only a few dim spotlights on so the place was dark, cold, and inhospitable.

Turning away from the raised platform, I noticed through the gloom some scaffolding that held about 15 rows of metal stadium-style seating.

'Did you know there was going to be an audience,' I asked SHE.

'What! You're kidding me,' she yelped. 'Did they tell me that and I've forgotten? I can't … I'm sure I would have remembered that little detail.'

'What do you want to do?'

'DO? The show must go on, mustn't it? Isn't that what I'm supposed to say?'

Midge returned looking surlier than ever. 'Arrigh' come wiv me, and wotch ou' for the wires,' she grunted. She took us to what they called the Green Room where there were some drinks and snacks. 'Whay in 'ere an Makeup will come fer yer,' she said to SHE. 'Not gonna 'av yer lookin' like that.'

'What did she mean by that remark?' said SHE when Midge had left the room.

'They probably just need to throw powder over you so that you don't glisten too much under the lights. I think I saw that on a TV documentary.'

'Right, if you say so, but I'd like to whack her across her head with her silly clipboard. Why is it that anyone in TV, even in the lowliest of lowly positions, feels superior to everyone else? Makes me want to Wallace and Gromit.'[24] At that moment a young woman walked in whose fashion sense I think can only be described as Grunge On Steroids. The creature from the swamp asked SHE to follow her to Makeup.

'Are *you* making me up?' SHE asked politely.

'Yeah,' replied the creature as she spat gum into her right hand and used what remained of her left sleeve for storage.

As she left, SHE turned to me and mouthed, 'Help me.' I sat myself on a worn red sofa with a drink and some chocolate biscuits and started trawling through a tabloid magazine. I needed to catch up on what publicists are feeding us for our *newstainment*. I'll be honest, much of my life is lived vicariously through the goings-on of celebs. Pretty soon, I'm sure, the dumbing down of the Western world will reach rock bottom, and then we'll wise up. What am I thinking? There is no bottom.

---

[24] London slang for something rhyming with Gromit. Wallace and Gromit are claymation characters invented by the brilliant Nick Park.

SHE returned looking gorgeous although the makeup was perhaps too heavy. 'Apparently, you need all of this junk to look natural,' she shrugged. 'Ironic, isn't it?'

The show's host – Mark Apple – followed behind her and shook her hand ever so softly. He was made up as well, and too vigorous a movement might have cracked his face.

'Sheila, absolutely terrific to be working with you. I just thought I would pop in to see if you have any questions. I know Nathan, our producer chappie, has discussed the format and questions with you. Any little thing I can help with?'

'There's going to be an audience,' said SHE. 'I don't remember having been told that.'

'Oh my, my. I'm positively sure Nathan must have done so. That's sooooo part of standard procedure. Don't worry about the mob, my dear. They don't do anything but sit there and add a little real-worldly atmosphere – laughter, clapping, stamping of feet, and so on. Just joking about the last one by the way. Strangely, we find an audience puts our guests at ease. Well, must be off to gargle and take the voice box out for a spin. It will be an absolutely super show. Trust me.' He waved his ultra-thin manicured fingers at us and wafted out of the room.

Before long Midge came back and turned on a TV standing in a corner. 'Yer c'n see wots goin' on from 'ere,' she said to me. 'Jus' keep yer 'ands off ov the fing. Ain't gonna buy any mor TVs fer yous lot.' I wasn't sure who *our lot* was, but I let it pass. I didn't want to add more pressure to what SHE was already feeling. Actually SHE looked quite calm; I was the one pacing the floor and spilling salsa and blue cheese dip down my shirt. Could I have caught the Sloppy Sadie Syndrome?

'Would you like a cup of coffee?' I asked SHE.

'That sounds good.'

I reached into my bag and pulled out a Caffeine Tornado. 'I'm afraid it's cold, but I thought perhaps …'

'Oh Will, that's so sweet. Thank you. How many do I owe you now?'

'Slate's clean.'

She had only taken a couple of sips when Midge came back.

'Les get yer wired up,' she said to SHE.

'Afterwards, let's send her a gift certificate for an emergency charm school,' SHE whispered to me.

Within a couple of minutes I could see her on the TV being seated in one of the leather chairs. A sound engineer asked her to thread the microphone wire up through her blouse and on to her jacket collar. It took a while to get the threading and sound checking done, but then she was ready to roll. Mark Apple came and sat opposite her and started a little small talk to put her at ease. Soon all was ready and some up-tempo techno music signalled the start of the recording.

'Hello and welcome to Inside Trends. I'm delighted this evening to have Sheila Hetherington-Etheridge with us, Managing Director of *The Fun House*, the maker of some of the world's most popular electronic games. Thanks for being with us Sheila.'

'My pleasure.'

'We're here to talk about the exciting global world of work, but before we do that, let's look at some of the footage we took recently on a visit to *The Fun House*.'

The next few minutes showed a tape of myself, Moonbeam, Sadie, Diceman, and others interacting with global team members via GO*dz*Willa. The idea was to show how a team, given all of the challenges of working across distances, could manage a project. Sometimes you could just hear voices of people like Robert Chang via VoIP, and at other times you could see us interacting via video with Sunil and Daavid. They also showed us interacting informally via IM in *The Wit's End Café*. Several of us were interviewed about working globally via technology. We had worked out beforehand that Sadie would talk about the challenges of global virtual working: Isolation, Fragmentation, and Confusion. I would talk about overcoming those challenges through increasing the levels of team Engagement, Cohesion, and Clarity, and we divided up talking about the Six Cs between SHE, the Diceman, and me. At the end of the film, Mark Apple turned back to SHE.

'Very, interesting. It's certainly a different world of work. Most of our parents, I suspect, wouldn't relate to it very much.'

'I know mine don't,' said SHE laughing.

'In the film clip we saw your *players*, as you call them, talking briefly about global collaboration in *The Fun House*.'

'Yes, we've condensed our approach into a visual for you.'

While SHE spoke, a slide I had been working on until the early hours of the morning appeared on the screen. It's clunky rather than stylish; bit like its creator!

'This is what we call our Collaboration Controller,' SHE explained.

'Like a game controller?' asked Apple.

'That's correct; it keeps our attention focused on the right buttons for our global virtual teamwork. Inside you can see what we call The Six Cs of Global Collaboration, and we look to continually improve these to raise the levels of team engagement, cohesion, and clarity and beat isolation, fragmentation, and confusion.'

'Why don't you take a little time and explain them to us, Sheila.'

'Certainly, but first let me say that these Six Cs are not just a concern for virtual teams. They apply to face-to-face teams as well. Virtual working just amplifies the difficulties and increases the negative consequences of neglect in any one of them. For example, face-to-face teams can often get away with fuzziness in coordination. Team members who are working together in the same space can usually spot gaps, overlaps, or a lack of clarity quite easily. With goodwill

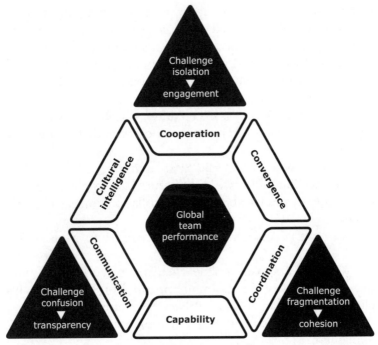

Collaboration Controller.

they can negotiate, make quick adjustments, and move on. When distance becomes a factor, it's not so easy. It's harder for us to know what others are doing in virtual space. Distance and silence often breed paranoia and resentment, for no valid reason. Confusion and misunderstandings are often submerged on virtual teams and create havoc.'

'So virtual teams need to be extra vigilant in putting the building blocks of collaboration in place?'

'That's right. Now, let me take you into the Six Cs starting with Cooperation. Our actions, right from the very beginning, will establish a cooperative climate, or not. We need to give and get trust from others quickly.'

'Not an easy task over distances, I'm sure,' interjected Apple.

'True, but if the leader-facilitator can model constructive and trusting behaviours at the beginning, that will go a long way to setting the right tone. We must give trust and get trust. You give trust through such actions as delegating responsibility and authority, and being open to sharing your knowledge and expertise with others. How do we get trust? We do things like responding quickly and thoughtfully to others, by keeping our promises, and by keeping views and issues in the team confidential.'

'I see, good to know.'

'Cooperation, however, is not enough. To avoid virtual team fragmentation and members losing their focus, we must converge around a common purpose, principles, a shared sense of direction, and agreement on priorities. If we don't, team cohesion is at risk and members will drift away to work on what interests them. To support convergence and alignment, we also need clear goals, objectives, plans, and performance indicators to act as additional markers to navigate by.'

Mark Apple is nodding so vigorously he looks like a toy with a wobbly head.

'Now, if cooperation and convergence are to add real collaborative value, the efforts of team members must be coordinated through clearly defined roles and responsibilities, shared tools, processes, systems, and methods. The efforts of the team must be synchronized or else team energy becomes scattered and unproductive.'

SHE paused for a quick sip of water, and then kept right on going. 'If a team is to fulfil the promise of its coordinated efforts it must be sure to build its capabilities. The knowledge, skills, and experiences of *all* members, no matter where they are located, need to be developed and combined. Knowledge and expertise are so critical to being competitive these days, none should be wasted.'

'Does *The Fun House* team do well at using everyone's knowledge and expertise?' asked Apple. Not a question I remember being discussed in the preparation phase.

'I think we do a pretty good job. We try to accommodate different styles in making contributions to the team.'

'Can you give us an example?'

'Yes. Some people prefer to put things in writing, others to talk. Some want to give instant feedback, others want to take time to process. Some are happy to be very public with their ideas while others would rather be anonymous. In our electronic Global Office Workspace – GO*dz*Willa as we call it – no one really has an excuse for not contributing his or her knowledge and expertise because the options for doing so are so varied.'

'GO*dz*Willa is the technology we saw your people using in the film?'

'That's right. It's the closest thing we have to a shared global workspace.'

'Great name.'

'We like it, but then we're a bit weird.'

'Weird in a good way, I think. But let's move on to communication.'

'Sure. In making the best use of our capabilities, we must get the right information to the right people at the right time in the right way and, very importantly, with a meaning shared by all. People cannot contribute well if they don't know what's going on or if they don't have the raw material to work with. Exchanging the information is not enough; communication only exists when there is shared understanding.'

'I'm so glad to hear you say that. It seems to me that technology is often just allowing us to communicate badly, more often,' said Apple, obviously pleased with his turn of phrase.

'True. Now, reaching shared understanding across borders depends on the last of the Six Cs, cultural intelligence. This is our ability to be inclusive of diverse value and style differences.'

Following SHE's overview of the Six Cs, Mark Apple focused attention on GO*dz*Willa and the technologies that were making global collaboration in *The Fun House* possible.

'The pace of technological change has been astounding,' SHE said, 'but the really important task is to make sure we are able to make the different technologies fit *our* needs rather than the other way around – to create an engaging virtual work environment that we feel excited to be in.'

'I'm sure it's challenging for many to hear *work* and *excited* in the same sentence,' said Apple.

'It shouldn't be. We're a maker of games, and so we tend to look at work as a collaborative game. I know some in business don't like thinking about what they do as game-like, but in essence it is. We agree on our shared *quest* and what the common rules are, and off we go. Every day we re-enter the game, look at where we left off, try to identify what gremlins might try to destroy us, and work together to overcome them and reach our goal.'

'Work sounds like fun when you put it like that.'

'Work is too serious not to be fun.'

'Explain that a little more for me, Sheila.'

'If work is stripped of fun, we have a hard time fully engaging with it, and if we don't fully engage, we're not taking our work seriously. Fun and work are complementary, not opposites.'

'This idea of work as a game – it sounds intriguing. How do you envisage the future?'

'I imagine a time in *The Fun House* when we enter project variables like team members, locations, objectives, resources, collaboration rules, and timeframes into a piece of software; the software then transforms the project into a game to be played by team members. No matter where in the world team members are, they will all be playing in the same game. Can you think of a more powerful way to create an engaged and cohesive virtual team?'

'Work is entering an altered state. Fascinating,' said Apple intently. 'But if you are working on several projects you could be playing in several different games.'

'You think that will be a problem for this generation? The average 21-year-old today has already spent 10 000 hours playing video games.'

'Truly fascinating,' said Apple, even more intently.

'We're also looking at setting up *The Fun House* HQ in a virtual world like *Second Life*. Regardless of location or project games we're playing in, we would all share the same virtual office space. I think our GO*dz*Willa is a step in that direction.'

'Remarkable. When can I join *The Fun House?*' asked Apple.

'E-mail me your CV,' said SHE laughing.

'What else can you see in your crystal ball?'

I could see SHE buying herself some time by taking another sip of water. 'In the not too distant future,' she went on, 'we might see brain–computer interfaces that enable electrical signals from the brain to control what is happening on the screen.[25] Imagine your avatar communicating your smiles and grimaces as you make them in the real world. Imagine an interface that senses your emotional states and makes modifications to your online environment. Or a user interface that can read your conscious intentions to push, pull, rotate, or lift something in the virtual world, or even smack someone over the head with a clipboard.' I nearly fell off the sofa laughing when I remembered what SHE had wanted to do to Midge. I wondered if Midge was growling on the set.

The discussion went on with Mark Apple continuing to be absolutely and totally fascinated. I was truly admiring of SHE who had Apple and the audience eating out of the palm of her hand.

'Tell me Sheila, you've given us the Six Cs for global collaboration and a fascinating glimpse into the future.

---

[25] Emotiv Systems, a San Francisco based electronic game company, is selling EEG (electroencephalograph) caps and toolkits for software developers. These enable games to be built that utilize electrical signals from a player's brain to manipulate action on the screen.

Are there any guidelines or general rules for working in this environment that you would like to leave our audience with?'

'Yes. To help us maximize performance as a team, we have developed 10 operating rules. These describe behaviours that contribute to the success of the team overall.'

A list of the 10 rules came up on the screen:

- Be Accessible – everyone to be virtually present and available as much as possible.
- Be Alert – everyone to be on the lookout in his or her 'world' for emerging trends, opportunities, and threats.
- Be Aligned – everyone to act consistently with others in following the agreed-upon virtual collaboration rules.
- Be Connected – everyone to reach out to others (inside and outside the team) with similar interests and issues.
- Be a Partner – everyone to exploit virtual tools and processes to share knowledge and skills.
- Be Innovative – everyone to apply their imagination to beating the virtual challenges of isolation, fragmentation, and confusion.
- Be Open – everyone to be receptive and broadminded about ideas that can appear culturally counterintuitive.
- Be Responsible – everyone to take personal ownership for team results.
- Be Thoughtful – everyone to show respect and consideration for others on the team.
- Be Transparent – everyone to keep their thinking and actions visible to the virtual others.

'Sheila, as you did with the Six Cs, perhaps you could quickly take our viewers through some of them.'

'Certainly. Being Alert. Everyone on the virtual team must be a sensor feeding back information to others. When each one of us finds sources of "food", or information in our case, we must enable everyone else to access the source so that the team as a whole benefits and becomes stronger. Like ants, we need to leave scent trails to "food" that will sustain the colony.'

'Interesting. What kind of scent trails?' said Apple.

'Oh, things like tags and links to interesting websites.'

'I see. Tell us about some more of the rules before our time runs out.'

'Another is Be Aligned, to act consistently with others in following the agreed upon rules. When there is consistency in applying the rules, the team acts as a powerful, collectively intelligent unit like a swarm, and not as isolated, relatively weak, individuals.'

'Next is Be Connected, reaching out to others with similar interests and issues. In gaming there is a huge community of people who are passionate and knowledgeable about games. They want to contribute to the evolution of games, and we enable them to do that. All the expertise doesn't need to be among players in *The Fun House.*'

SHE stopped to take another sip of water from her mug. During the brief silence, someone in the audience dropped what sounded like a small oil drum. It rolled and clanked from the top of the metal seating to the bottom. The heavy clattering caused the audience to let out a collective gasp and swivel in all directions looking for the culprit.

I thought Midge was going to leap into the audience and start beating someone up. Apple stepped in quickly. 'Stop tape. Let's pick it up from Be Connected. Sorry Sheila. You're doing brilliantly. It may sound like you're doing a lot of continuous talking, but don't worry about it. We'll be editing in more film clips as you speak to keep it lively. Control Room, you ready my loves?' A furious Midge gave a keep rolling sign. 'Start again when you're ready Sheila,' said Apple, 'that's the beauty of not being live.' I was wondering how SHE would react to the interruption, but she didn't blink an eyelid.

'Two important rules when we're working across cultures,' she said, 'are Be Open and Be Thoughtful. Sometimes you might hear someone from another culture present an idea that doesn't fit with your current mental model of how the world works. In *The Fun House*, we are always challenging each other to stay open and live with the ambiguity and uncertainty for a while. The idea might be a real golden nugget.'

'Be Thoughtful can cover many areas. For example, keeping your language simple and precise, sharing the burden of having to meet at unfriendly hours, sending people something in advance of a meeting so that they can read and absorb before having to speak about it. That's especially important for people whose first language is not English.'

'Yes, I could see how that could be very helpful. Just share one more with us.'

'OK. I think the Be Transparent rule is critical to success on a virtual team. So much frustration and anxiety is caused when we constantly have to second-guess each other. So much potentially productive time is wasted when we are trying to read minds.'

'Any last minute advice before we close?' said Apple.

'Don't forget that on a virtual team whatever you're doing should be contributing to raising the levels of Engagement, Cohesion, and Clarity. Make those three words your mantra.'

'Excellent. On that note, I'm afraid we're going to have to bring things to a close. Sheila, it's been delightful having you here. We wish you and *The Fun House* every success as you create the future. For our viewers, you can go to our website and see this programme again or purchase a transcript. Until next week when we will be looking at exciting new trends in sewage treatment – yes, you don't want to miss that one. It is a very good night from me, Mark Apple.'

When the closing music started to play, I rushed from the Green Room to the set. SHE was shaking hands with Apple who was congratulating her on a great show. When SHE saw me she held out her arms and gave me a bear hug.

'How did I do, Will?' she asked breathlessly.

'You were absolutely … amazing. You looked like you had been doing TV forever. Brilliant!'

'Thank you for everything, Will,' she whispered into my ear, and then she kissed me on the cheek. While we hugged, I looked over her shoulder towards the audience. Most of them were leaving through an exit at the back of the studio, but one small, dark figure was aggressively pushing against the flow and towards the stage. The figure drew closer and came under the spotlights. Seeing was not believing – it was the demonette of darkness herself, PAULA! She looked to be carrying a large aerosol can of spray paint which I'm sure was not for brightening up the studio decor.

I grabbed Sheila's hand and shouted hysterically, 'Now … quick … come on!' I yanked her off the set and through a pair of double doors, trying desperately to remember the way we had come in.

'Will, what are you doing? For God's sake, what's the matter? My stuff is in the Green Room,' she said, frantically trying to pull me in that direction.

'I'll come back for it,' I panted. 'No time … absolutely no time.'

I pulled her down a set of stairs to an exit that took us on to a dark side street. It was pelting with rain and the lashing wind was easily gale force.

Bolting into the main road, I caught sight of a taxi rank across the street. Unceremoniously, I shoved SHE through the door of the nearest cab and on to the back seat, landing on top of her as I did so.

'Where to guv?' said the cabbie.

'Anywhere. Just drive.'

'Whatever. Jus' behave yerself back there or I'll have the police on yer,' he chuckled.

Glancing out the back window, I was just in time to see Midge rugby tackle Paula in the street. The well-timed assault landed both of them in a streaming torrent of water cascading along the gutter. Midge, I'm sure, was highly miffed that someone had interrupted the recording. I almost stopped the taxi so that I could truly enjoy the moment – maybe take a picture on my phone for later posting on the web. Suddenly

I remembered that I was sprawled across SHE and probably suffocating her. I climbed off and wondered how I was going to explain myself.

SHE looked at me, her thick makeup running in lava streams down her cheeks, and her soaked blonde hair hanging like forlorn lettuce leaves. 'Will ... Will, this is all very flattering my love,' she gasped as she unclamped my hand from hers, 'but you do know I'm gay, don't you?'

I saw the driver's eyes dart up to his rearview mirror in amused anticipation of what might happen next. I felt totally at a loss. Pathetically, the only thing I could think of doing was to shake her hand while saying, 'Really? That's nice. Good for you.'

The small traffic pile-up that followed wasn't that serious, but the embarrassing headline in next day's tabloid read, CABBIE, WHO NEARLY DIED LAUGHING, BLAMES FRUSTRATED HOT LOVER FOR CRASH. ... The passenger William Williams of Camden Town ... blah, blah, B ... L ... A ... H!

How to explain this one to Sophie?

BRIEFING REPORT: GLOBAL VIRTUAL TEAM ESSENTIALS

To: Sheila Hetherington-Etheridge
From: Will Williams
Purpose
This report summarizes my findings on the new workplace.

SECTION 1: THE NEW WORKPLACE

Two key characteristics of the new workplace are that it is:

Virtual: people are working together via technologies, in virtual spaces rather than face-to-face.
Global: colleagues and partners are often working from many different parts of the world.

Why is this new workplace evolving now?

Key drivers:

- Globalization, reducing the influence of commercial and labour borders.
- New communications and computing technologies, enabling a global workplace.

Resulting in:

- Increased levels of complexity, uncertainty, ambiguity, and paradox.

That can only be managed by:

- Intensive and extensive collaboration across internal and external borders.

Meaning:

- Competitive advantage is increasingly tied to collaborative advantage developed in virtual space.

SECTION 2: CHALLENGES, COUNTERMEASURES, AND TEAM PERFORMANCE ZONES

Three major challenges of virtual collaboration are:

Isolation: as a result of reduced contact, restricted social cues, difficulty of trust-building, reduced sense of team identity, and the out-of-sight/out-of-mind syndrome.

Fragmentation: as a result of unclear purpose, fuzzy roles and responsibilities, local pressures and priorities, uncertainties around decision making, neglect of finding common ground.

Confusion: as a result of too much or too little communication, imprecise communication, lack of shared contextual understanding, conflicting assumptions, activities hidden from one another by distance.

These challenges can have an impact on face-to-face teams also, but distance and reduced contact tend to magnify them. To counteract these challenges, a virtual team needs to generate high levels of:

Engagement: emotional involvement and commitment to the work of the team.

Cohesion: working together as a unified, coordinated whole.

Clarity: shared understandings across the team.

How will the team generate high levels in these three areas? It needs to focus attention on six team performance zones:

Cooperation: ability to develop and maintain trusting relationships across geographies, time zones, and cultures.

Convergence: ability to maintain a clear purpose, direction, and shared set of priorities.

Coordination: ability to align work through clearly defined roles and responsibilities, shared tools, processes, and methods.

Capability: ability to leverage knowledge, skills, and experiences of all members, and increase the capabilities of the team as a whole.

Communication: ability to generate shared verbal and written understandings across distances via technology.

Cultural Intelligence: ability to develop and maintain a global virtual workplace inclusive of value and style differences.

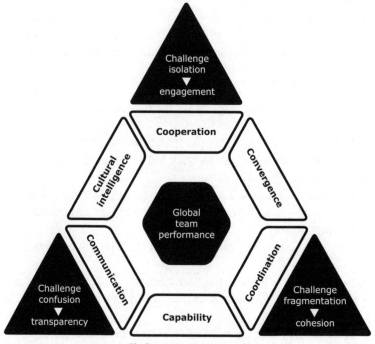

Collaboration Controller.

SECTION 3: COOPERATION

Virtual Trust

What is the need?

To develop the confidence that team colleagues who work with you primarily via technology can be trusted and relied upon (despite challenges such as distances, different time zones, and cultures), to meet or exceed expectations in working towards shared goals.

Why is it important?

Leaders of distributed virtual teams cannot hope to be effective through command and control mechanisms. They can set a strategic direction and negotiate guidelines and expectations, but effective performance relies heavily on trust and communication.

Pathways to Virtual Trust

Several factors help contribute to developing trust on the team: Having the Right Mindset; Understanding the Context; Paying Attention to Behaviours; Paying Attention to Process.

Having the Right Mindset

- Respect – treating others with consideration and appreciation.
- Openness – being receptive to all ideas.
- Honesty – being straightforward; having no hidden agendas.
- Integrity – demonstrating honesty, fairness; being unbiased.
- Empathy – understanding others and their circumstances; feeling affinity.
- Caring – showing consideration for the well-being of others.
- Confidence – having trust in oneself.
- Congeniality – being sociable, friendly, and pleasant to work with.
- Reciprocity – being willing to share; give and take.

Understanding the Context

The Situation

- Complexity Level – understanding the difficulties inherent in the task.
- Risk Level – understanding the consequences if the team fails.

If the complexity of the task is high and the risk level is high, the team is unlikely to build trust until the competence and reliability of team members has been demonstrated.

The Players

- Self Awareness – awareness of one's own biases in making a trust decision.
- Other Awareness – awareness of how others perceive trustworthiness.

The Challenges

- Environmental – understanding potential barriers outside the organization and how they could impact on the team's work and relationships.
- Organizational – understanding potential barriers inside the organization and how they could impact on the team.
- Technological – understanding how the use of different technologies helps or hinders the development of trusting relationships.
- Operational – understanding how different perceptions of goals, roles, and processes can impact on relationships.
- Geographical – understanding how distance can contribute to isolation, fragmentation, and confusion, and consequently to the growth of distrust.
- Cultural – understanding how differences in values, beliefs, and behaviours can impact on the development of trusting relationships.

Paying Attention to Behaviours

Giving Trust
- Suspending doubt about trustworthiness; trust but verify.
- Sharing knowledge and expertise to demonstrate good faith and develop goodwill.
- Delegating authority to demonstrate confidence in others.

Getting Trust
- Being present and accessible to everyone to demonstrate participation and commitment.
- Responding quickly and thoughtfully to others to show engagement.
- Keeping promises to demonstrate dependability.
- Being predictable to demonstrate consistency.
- Being flexible to show adaptability to change.
- Being enthusiastic and optimistic to demonstrate commitment.
- Listening and paying attention to demonstrate respect and openness.
- Demonstrating competence to show reliability.
- Giving support to demonstrate caring and empathy.
- Handling conflict constructively to demonstrate calmness.
- Communicating even when you don't have to demonstrate sociability.
- Keeping confidentiality to demonstrate integrity.
- Being inclusive to demonstrate impartiality.
- Refusing to talk behind people's backs to demonstrate fairness.
- Solving problems rather than assigning blame to demonstrate pragmatism.
- Setting challenging but realistic expectations to demonstrate common sense.
- Taking the initiative to demonstrate confidence.

Paying Attention to Relationship Building
- Forming – the phase of early relationship building and preliminary task and operational analysis.

- Transitioning – the phase of testing each other and negotiating through differences in perceptions, styles, and methods to create shared understandings and expectations.
- Developing – the phase of deepening trusting relationships through frequent and rich communication and interaction, sharing, and mutual support.

General Pointers for Building Cooperation

- Meet face-to-face early in the life of the team (if at all possible) to build relationships, shared ownership and personal commitment; meet face-to-face at regular intervals if you can.
- At the beginning of a project focus on establishing relationships, and not just assigning tasks; promote a shared sense of identity and belonging.
- Establish a climate of enthusiastic, open, honest, and respectful communication in which all ideas are valued, listened to, and explored.
- Quickly demonstrate your capabilities, your integrity, and your caring for others.
- Maintain a sense of presence through frequent and thoughtful communications, and fast responses.
- Problem-solve rather than assign blame; deal with problems in a calm, confident way.
- Establish transparency, keeping promises, confidentiality, and mutual accountability as key operating principles.
- Develop shared understanding of the different contexts in which team members are working: the local constraints.
- Keep the whole project visible to team members, not just the parts.
- Work together to determine the best way to handle conflict on the team.
- Recognize and celebrate the achievements of the team.

SECTION 4: CONVERGENCE

What is the need?

To provide guidance markers in virtual space to enable the team to 'lock-on' to a common sense of where the team is, where it is going, and how it is going to get there. While there can be many perspectives and styles on global virtual teams, its members need one-line-of-sight, one reason for being.

Why is this important?

Because of distance and the 'pressure of the local', global virtual teams face exponentially increased risks of team fragmentation, suboptimization, and focus drift. Teams with a sharp focus on their purpose often beat teams who have more expertise, skills, and resources.

What do global virtual teams need to do?

They need to develop and maintain clear markers for navigation in virtual space, such as:

Purpose: a shared understanding of the team's reason for being.

Principles: negotiated agreements for how team members will behave towards one another in order to achieve their purpose.

For example:

- Respect
- Honesty
- Keeping promises
- Handling conflict constructively
- Accountability

Priorities: a shared view of what things are most important, taking into account global and local contexts.

Plan: an agreed course of action with clear goals/objectives, timeframes and responsibilities.

Performance Indicators: agreed measures for monitoring team progress, e.g. levels of Engagement, Cohesion, and

Clarity. The team should also have task-related performance indicators.

General Pointers for Developing Convergence

- Work together – ideally face-to-face – to create a single team purpose statement, team principles, strategy plan, high-level priorities, and measures that make them explicit and tangible. Face-to-face team participation will help build shared ownership and personal commitment.
- Make sure that all members share exactly the same understanding of the team purpose, etc.
- Eliminate activities nonaligned with purpose, etc.
- Always be on the lookout for surface alignment that actually hides team members on different tracks
- Uncover and manage local demands that could take team members off-purpose.
- Revisit the team purpose, strategy plan, and priorities, etc., on a regular basis to ensure shared understanding and continued validity.

SECTION 5: COORDINATION

What is the need?

To create a shared virtual workspace that enables users to optimize the benefits of both of the following:

Predictability: in activities that demand consistent application of common templates, tools, processes, systems, and roles, e.g. planning, finance, and quality control.

Unpredictability: in activities that demand a degree of creativity, spontaneity, and serendipity, e.g. research and development, design, and marketing.

Why is it important?

One type of coordination space doesn't work for all teams at all times. Teams need to continuously calibrate their coordination activities to the goals they are trying to accomplish at different points in time, i.e. they must continuously adjust to find their coordination *sweet spot*.

Team activities and virtual coordination spaces.

Primary activity	Aim for a coordination space that promotes
Innovation	**Openness** • Brainstorming • Researching • Playing with ideas • Communicating across organizational and other borders
Planning	**Definition** • Analysing and consolidating • Goal and objective setting • Task, process, and milestone analysis • Critical path and strategy mapping • Role and responsibility clarity
Execution	**Synchronization** Collaboration – synchronous and asynchronous Formal and regular communication Spontaneous communication Reporting and logging Performance monitoring and feedback Team memory access

Coordination Options

Top Down – prescriptions from the top levels of the hierarchy about how coordination will be accomplished.

Bottom Up – application of shared behavioural rules developed/evolved by team members for optimizing their coordinated efforts.

Global teams are likely to have a blend of the two coordination approaches, although increasing emphasis is being place on bottom up, co-created rules.

Useful Behavioural Rules for Bottom Up Coordination

• Be Accessible – keep the communication channels as open as possible.

- Be Alert – always be on the lookout for emerging trends, opportunities, and threats.
- Be Aligned – act consistently with others in following the rules.
- Be Connected – reach out to others with similar interests and issues.
- Be Informative – always share what you know.
- Be Innovative – identify problems, solve them, learn, and keep going.
- Be Present – show others you are there with them as much as possible.
- Be Responsible – take personal ownership and take action.
- Be Thoughtful – show consideration for others on the team.
- Be Transparent – keep your thinking and actions visible to everyone.

Some Useful Coordination Features for a Global Workspace

- People representations (avatars).
- Presence tools – who's online, who's not, who is expected and when, etc.?
- Personal information sharing tools – what am I doing, thinking, and why?
- Personal profiles with knowledge, skills, and experience information.
- Shared diary with request for meeting capability.
- Asynchronous communication tools, e.g. e-mail, threaded discussions, wikis.
- Synchronous communication tools, e.g. VOiP, instant web conferencing.
- Global clock and meeting planner.
- Instant web meeting facility.
- Time logs.

- Immediate access to current project plans, budgets, progress dashboards, etc.
- Maps of work interdependencies and critical paths.
- Coupling tools whereby information from different locations can be gathered.
- Live feeds of useful information.
- Language translation tools.
- Cultural awareness database and tools.
- Anonymous feedback areas.
- Online training modules for personal and professional development.
- Intelligent software agents.
- Open source creativity development area.
- Community of interest/practice enablers.
- Easily accessible toolboxes containing useful templates, job aids, etc.

General Pointers for Building Coordination
- Create a team charter of key operating principles and agreements.
- Breakdown large teams into smaller and temporary task teams.
- Create a contact list with time zone information.
- Agree on one online calendar for the whole team.
- Clearly define roles and responsibilities, and review them on a periodic basis.
- Create a role locator and interface map – who does what and who with?
- Create a responsibility matrix with clear decision-making guidelines.
- Map goals, objectives, associated tasks, and timings by subgroup and/or individual.
- Clearly map key processes shared by team members. Are there process owners?
- Create a resource-planning template.
- Monitor progress and ensure continuous feedback.

SECTION 6: CAPABILITY

What is the need?

To develop and make best use of the diverse knowledge, skills, and experiences of distributed team members to produce best-in-class results.

Why is it important?

Increasingly, global competitiveness is based on generating, sharing, and applying knowledge across borders.

Key Roles in Knowledge Processing on the Team

Constructive roles for leveraging the knowledge skills and experiences on the team can be divided into two categories: the Disturbers and the Mobilizers:

The Disturbers

- **Questioners:** those who keep asking probing questions.
- **Originators:** those who keep creating and innovating.
- **Transformers:** those who develop existing knowledge.
- **Seekers:** those who keep hunting for and gathering new knowledge.
- **Experimenters:** those who keep trying different things to see what works.

The Mobilizers

- **Accelerators:** those who transfer knowledge rapidly.
- **Amplifiers:** those who make sure everyone knows.
- **Channellers:** those who keep the distribution channels in good shape.
- **Implementers:** those who apply knowledge to produce tangible results.
- **Integrators:** those who identify valuable linkages.
- **Multipliers:** those who use knowledge to generate new possibilities.
- **Prioritizers:** those who focus knowledge generation and application on critical areas.

- **Sense Makers:** those who interpret and translate for shared understanding.
- **Validators:** those who keep testing the robustness of new knowledge.

There are, of course, those who play roles that have negative effects: the Destructors.

The Destructors

- **Escalators:** those who create and fuel destructive communication spirals.
- **Hoarders:** those who keep knowledge to themselves.
- **Charlatans:** those who pretend to have expertise, but don't.
- **Chaotics:** those without discipline or organization.
- **Blockers:** those who create unnecessary barriers.
- **Toxics:** those who destroy the will to cooperate.
- **Whirling Dervishes:** those who cannot stay focused.

The Leader's Role in Developing Team Capabilities

The leader should make sure that he or she:

Energizes: *minimizes the potential demotivational impact of distance*: is a stable presence without micromanaging; has frequent virtual interactions with the team; keeps everyone informed; helps the team see the big picture; updates the team on performance in relation to goals; involves the team in key discussions about strategy and other issues; lets the team know of relevant outside developments; celebrates successes; talks with individuals, not just the team as a whole.

Enables: *creates the conditions in which team members can function autonomously and interdependently*: ensures clarity around goals, roles, standards, processes, etc.; helps minimize organizational barriers such as functional boundaries; helps establish team norms and shared working practices.

Empowers: *facilitates the work of the team rather than controlling*: identifies team member strengths and developmental areas; encourages team members to take on leadership responsibilities; reduces fear of taking the initiative; coaches rather than instructs.

Useful Questions for the Leader in Optimizing Knowledge Work Expertise:

Who on the team has it, if anyone?
Who can get it?
Who can create it?
Who wants to learn it?
Who needs it?
Who is in the best position to share it?
Who is in the best position to keep it updated?
Who can build on it?
Who can make it usable?
Who can best apply it?

Individual Attributes to Support Team Capability Development
Think TRADITIONS:

T = Technological Competence

- High comfort level with available technologies.
- Selects the best technology for the job to be done.
- Can troubleshoot and fix small problems.
- Knows when not to use technology.

R = Results-Orientation

- Stays focused on achieving team goals and objectives.
- Drives to get things done, makes things happen.
- Is always focused on adding value, not just being busy.

A = Accountability

- Takes responsibility for completing own work on time and within budget.
- Ensures work is done to highest possible standards.

- Takes responsibility for reconciling team needs and priorities with local demands.

D = Discipline
- Stays focused on priorities.
- Establishes and applies personal routines for managing own work flow.
- Seeks to minimize disruption to others and transferring of problems.

I = Initiative
- Takes calculated risks for the benefit of the team.
- Doesn't always wait for permission before acting.
- Is proactive in solving foreseeable problems.

T = Time Management
- Responds to others in a timely way.
- Prioritizes work to make the most positive impact.
- Meets deadlines.
- Sets personal boundaries to avoid being overextended.

I = Interpersonal Effectiveness
- Communicates simply and precisely.
- Listens attentively and gives clear, thoughtful responses.
- Appreciates the challenges of others' working environments.
- Ability to identify personal style and cultural differences and adapt well.
- Recognizes the value of differences to innovation and knowledge generation.
- Works collaboratively and constructively with others.

O = Openness
- Is welcoming of ideas from all sources.
- Demonstrates a willingness to share own expertise.
- Demonstrates flexibility.

N = Networking
- Reaches out to others inside and outside the team to expand knowledge and relationship base.
- Stays connected to other team members.

S = Self-Sufficiency

- Can work in relative isolation with little direct supervision.
- Tolerates ambiguity and uncertainty and works through it.
- Is self-reflective and takes responsibility for continuous professional development.

General Pointers for Building Capability

- Establish a continuous learning mindset and process.
- Conduct an informal Capability Audit so that members know what current knowledge, skills, and experiences are on the team.
- Provide opportunities for team member knowledge and skill development, e.g. project management, use of collaborative technologies, communication skills.
- Create virtual or face-to-face opportunities for identifying and sharing of best practices.
- Recognize and reward new knowledge generation across the team.
- Encourage all team members to take on leadership responsibilities based on experience, expertise, and personal career objectives.

SECTION 7: COMMUNICATION

What is the need?

To best use new technologies to create shared verbal, written, and visual understandings.

Why is it important?

Geographic and cultural distances magnify the chances for misunderstanding.

Challenges of Virtual Communication and Solution Sources

Most of the challenges related to virtual communication can be traced to there being Too Much of something (e.g. too much information from too many sources demanding too much attention) or Too Little of something (e.g. too infrequent communication, causing members to disengage).

Information challenges and solution sources.

In seeking solutions, teams need to be asking:

- How can we use the technologies to solve the problems they create, e.g. through finding, analysing, filtering, and prioritizing?
- What changes in behaviour will help eliminate or minimize the challenges, e.g. new routines, protocols, and disciplines?

General Pointers for Enabling Global Team Communication

- Create a formal communications plan.
- Encourage spontaneity and networking
- Communicate one-on-one, not just with the whole team.
- Be flexible, but communicate your own communication preferences.
- Identify your key touch points (KTPs).
- Add personality, enthusiasm, and warmth.
- Vary use of collaborative technologies.

Some Guidelines for Verbal Communications

- Slow down.
- Give people time to talk.
- Give people time to confer with others.
- Keep it simple.
- Save time and your sanity by doubling your communication efforts.
- Be honest.
- Pay close attention to what is said and not said.
- Check for shared meaning.
- Consolidate understanding.
- Ask straightforward questions.
- Add personality, enthusiasm, and warmth.

Some Guidelines for Written Communications

- Explain background context.
- Be exact.
- Be concise.
- Write carefully.
- Be restrained.
- Use visual and numerical anchors.
- Look at the message behind the words, the subtext.
- Treat written messages as permanent.

Communication Behaviours to Promote Engagement

- On large teams create subteams.
- Develop a communication rhythm while also being spontaneous.
- Begin with social communications and then work towards the task.
- Encourage social networking.
- Communicate one-on-one and not just one-to-many.
- Promote a sense of mutual ownership and accountability.
- Put personality into your communications.

- Use inclusive rather than exclusive language – 'we' rather than 'I'.
- As a role model be supportive and committed.
- Develop turn-taking norms so everyone's views are heard.
- Provide different methods for contributing: verbal, written, anonymous.
- Handle conflict constructively; problem solve.
- Have fun when communicating with each other.

Communication Behaviours to Promote Cohesion
- Reinforce purpose, goals, and objectives regularly.
- Work together on values to guide team interactions.
- Create set of shared norms for communication.
- Provide feedback regularly.
- Document important features of the team, e.g. roles and responsibilities, workflow.
- Create a shared plan of autonomous and interdependent work.
- Uncover and manage differences in technology/software platforms.
- Provide opportunities for sharing best practices and knowledge.
- Challenge any indications of 'the not invented here' syndrome.
- Challenge the formation of cliques that could trap information and resources.

Communication Behaviours to Promote Clarity
- Make sure expectations are clear.
- Quickly document and distribute main outputs from meetings.
- Create a team memory bank.
- Create a common vocabulary of key terms for use by the team.
- Make sure shared information is up-to-date and timely.

- Listen, be open. Ask questions, paraphrase, summarize – and often.
- Keep decision-making processes and outcomes clearly visible to all.
- Help team members understand the 'big picture'.
- Encourage open dialogue in which mutual understanding and learning is valued.
- Make cultural differences visible so they can be leveraged/managed effectively.

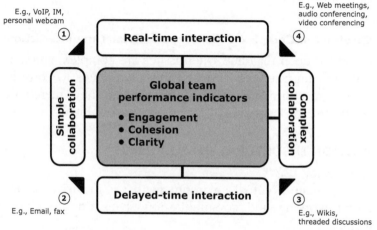

Match the right technology to the right job.

Quadrant 1: Simple Collaboration – Real-Time Interaction

Good for solving relatively easy problems one-to-one or one-to-few, or getting a quick decision. Useful as relationship starter/maintainer, giving personal feedback, solving lower-level conflicts, especially if used with webcam. Supportive of Engagement.

Quadrant 2: Simple Collaboration – Delayed-Time Interaction

Good for exchanges of unambiguous, structured, information. If information is ambiguous or it is critical to develop shared meaning, supplement with Quadrant 4 technologies. Supportive of Cohesion and Clarity.

Quadrant 3: Complex Collaboration – Delayed-Time Interaction

Good for having multiple perspectives build on one another over time; allows for reflection and convergence of thinking without the excessive to and fro of multiple e-mails and time-consuming synthesis. Supportive of Engagement, Cohesion, and Clarity.

Quadrant 4: Complex Collaboration – Real-Time Interaction

Good for open dialogue when issues are complex, ambiguous, and unstructured or when the team needs to consolidate, agree on a way forward, or welcome new members. Supportive of Engagement, Cohesion, and Clarity.

SECTION 8: CULTURAL INTELLIGENCE

What is the need?

To create a virtual environment that is inclusive of different working and communication styles on the global team.

Why is it important?

A global team is a place where different cultures, styles, and approaches intersect; it is at the intersections where creativity and new values can be discovered.

The RISK™ Framework of Cultural Intelligence

R = Recognize: cultural differences influencing interactions on the team.

I = Impact: understand the impact of those differences on working together.

S = Strategize: select an appropriate way for managing differences for best results.

K = Know-how: apply self-management know-how to support cross-border collaboration.

Recognizing Differences

Utilizing the Worldprism™ model of cultural differences is a way to help identify the diverse cultural orientations on the team.

The Worldprism™ model.

Cultural area	Cultural orientations	
RELATING Expectations on how to interact appropriately with others	**Task** Impersonal. Let's get down to business. Rules before relationships	**Relationship** Personal. Can I trust you? Are you loyal? Relationships before rules
	Explicit Meaning is stated directly. Say what you mean and mean what you say	**Implicit** Meaning often has to be inferred from what is said *and* not said, and body language
	Individual Me before we	**Group** We before me
REGULATING Expectations on how to manage our work together	**Risk Taking** Make change happen; act decisively. New is good	**Risk Avoiding** Avoid change. Steady, but sure. Stress continuity
	Tight Be punctual, control time. Time is money	**Loose** Be flexible, go with the flow. Things will happen in their own time
	Shared Distribute power and authority within the group	**Concentrated** Focus power and authority on specific people in the group

The Worldprism™ model. (continued)

Cultural area	Cultural orientations	
REASONING Expectations on how to think about problems and present solutions	**Linear** Analytical, step-by-step process towards solution	**Circular** Focus on exploring and integrating perspectives in arelatively unstructured way
	Facts Emphasis on data and concrete experiences	**Thinking** Emphasis on reasoning, concepts, and logic
	Simple Focus on essentials with little context	**Complex** Focus on developing a detailed, contextual understanding

Strategic Options for Working with Cultural Differences

Adapt: We adjust behaviours to accommodate one another.

Blend: The best approach is a mix of your way and my way.

Co-create: Together we'll develop a new way that works for all of us.

Divide: You do it your way, I'll do it mine. The differences don't have a negative impact.

Enforce: We have to do things this way. We have no choice.

Self-Management: Common Mistakes Made When Working Across Cultures

Lack of control over potentially damaging:

Feelings	Thoughts	Behaviours
For example:	*For example:*	*For example:*
• Anger	• Bias	• Aggression
• Anxiety	• Ethnocentrism	• Arrogance
• Aversion	• Denial	• Domination
• Cynicism	• Judging	• Inflexibility
• Frustration	• Minimizing	• Insensitivity
• Impatience	• Projecting	• Unreliability
• Mistrust	• Stereotyping	• Disinterest

A Self-Management Process: Prepare – Act – Check – Apply (PACA)

Prepare: research likely differences you will encounter; avoid surprises and you can adjust more easily, as well as set more realistic expectations.

Act: act on your learned knowledge and understanding of a culture.

Check: check on others' reactions and your own – in real-time.

Apply: apply what you are learning in real-time; keep checking your own and others' responses and adjust.

General Pointers for Using Cultural Intelligence

- Set realistic objectives and timeframes. Working across cultures often means people will be working outside existing comfort zones.
- Be careful of denying or minimizing differences. Respect differences by recognizing them.
- Work at developing cultural self-awareness. There are two sides to adaptation: adapting to and adapting from. We usually pay more attention to what we are adapting to, forgetting that to do that effectively we need to know our own starting point.
- Prepare yourself, but remain open. Learn what you might expect in working with people from the other culture(s), but focus on knowing the individuals you will be working with rather than the 'culture' *per se.*
- Try not to create resistance by working against the underlying values and beliefs of the other culture. Be creative in finding ways to work with them.
- Focus on leveraging differences to create value rather than simply trying to avoid cross-cultural mistakes.
- Keep learning about others. Developing cultural intelligence is an ongoing challenge and reward.

USEFUL TERMS

For those still wrestling with the new workplace

Agent   See Bots.

Aggregator   Software that gathers information
                     (typically news) from multiple
                     websites, usually via RSS feeds. The
                     information is reconfigured and
                     channelled to suit the needs of a
                     user, e.g. receiving the news specific
                     to a user-chosen keyword. Examples
                     of aggregators include: NewsIsFree,
                     Google Reader, FeedDemon
                     (Windows), NetNewsWire (Mac OS),
                     Feedview (cross-platform).

Asynchronous   Communication that takes place at
                     different times, e.g. via e-mail,
                     threaded discussions, or wikis.

Augmented Reality

Take a pair of today's eyeglasses through which you see the real-world in real-time. Now imagine that what you see through those eyeglasses is enhanced with informative graphics. Not only that, but the graphics change depending on your head and eye movements. Or imagine pointing your cell phone camera at a building, and your phone being able to give you information about that building.

Avatar

A representation/icon of a participant in a virtual world. The term comes from a Hindi Sanskrit word (*avatāra*) for a deity in visible form.

Blog

A web page allowing the creator (blogger) to instantly publish information to the Internet. Originally the term was short for 'weblog'. While the majority of blogs have been text-based, there are now audioblogs (podcasts), videoblogs, and photoblogs. Create your own at www. blogger.com. Blogs are being used within companies to promote communication and knowledge sharing.

Blogosphere

The universe of blogs. Also relates to the growing subculture of bloggers.

Blogroll

Other sites recommended by a blogger. They are usually located in a sidebar of a blog.

Bots	A software 'robot' for performing time-intensive activities (also known as software agents). Examples include search bots, tracking bots, and shopping bots. Copernic Agent Professional conducts searches on the different Internet search engines. See www.botspot.com.
Collaboration Readiness	The willingness and ability of a group to pool expertise and other resources for accomplishing a shared goal.
Collaboration Technology Readiness	Having the right functionality, user willingness, and competencies in place to exploit fully the available collaborative tools and technologies.
Collaborative Software	See Groupware.
Collaboratory	A networked community of scientists who collaborate with colleagues in a virtual research environment, thereby making more efficient and effective use of resources. The idea of forming a collaboratory is now moving beyond the scientific community.
Collocated	Being physically present in the same space.

Continuous Partial Attention — A state of being in which one's attention is always fragmented. The focus of our attention might be on a primary task, but we are also checking on others in the background for fear of missing something important to us.

Co-presence — The feeling of being together with another person(s) even when at a distance from one another.

Crowdsourcing — Applying the principles and practices of open sourcing (see Open Source) to fields outside software development.

Cultural Co-creation — Negotiating shared norms and operating agreements for collaborating.

Cultural Intelligence — The ability to recognize cultural differences and how they potentially impact on one another, while also applying appropriate strategies and self-management techniques to achieve mutually beneficial goals.

Cultural Orientation — Group preference for a different aspect of a cultural dimension, e.g. preference for direct over indirect communication, shared over concentrated power.

Culture Flexing — Adapting to one or more of the cultural orientations exhibited by another person(s).

Deindividuation   A process by which we lose our
individual self-awareness and self-
restraint. In a virtual group we can
feel more anonymous and
start acting out of character, e.g. more
aggressively.

Digital   Signs of nonverbal behaviour in
Nonverbals   synchronous and written
communications, use of emoticons
like :oP and acronyms (LOL, brb).

Employee Portal   A B2E (Business to Employee)
productivity tool. Provides distributed
employees with a single Web-enabled
interface for accessing applications
and company information.

Extranet   Basically, an intranet that allows
different levels of access to those
outside the organization, e.g.
customers, partners. Identity
determines what parts can be viewed.

Firewall   Security filter to protect computers/
networks from unauthorized access.

Folksonomy   A user-generated taxonomy for
categorizing and retrieving content on
the web.

Globally   Work dispersed across countries,
Distributed   economies, and national/
Work   organizational cultures.
Workers are in different locations and
primarily communicating via
asynchronous technologies.

Groupware

A generic name for programs that help people collaborate across distances, e.g. calendar sharing, electronic meetings, shared database access. May also be called collaborative software.

HCI

Academic field studying Human–Computer Interaction.

Hotspot

Location offering access to Wi-Fi.

Intranet

A secure private computer network based on Internet technology that resides behind an organization's firewall.

In-world

Being inside a virtual world.

Life Cast

Using digital media and the Internet to broadcast one's own life as it happens.

Mashup

Putting different tools together to create something new, e.g. ChicagoCrime.org mashes together data from the Chicago Police Department with Google Maps.

Metaverse

A term coined by Neal Stephenson in his cyberpunk novel *Snow Crash*. It refers to the emerging virtual reality-based or 3D Internet, an immersive environment where you would shop, for example, in 3D stores rather than on the current flat pages. See www. metaverseroadmap.org.

Microblogging   Service enabling a user to write brief text updates to a profile page that can be sent to others (via website, IM, SMS, RSS, or e-mail) who have signed up to receive them. Services include Twitter and Jaiku.

MMORPGs   Massively Multiplayer Online Role-Playing Games. These online games like 'World of Warcraft' often have many thousands of players at a time, from across the globe, interacting with one another in a persistent world (see Persistent World). Companies like IBM and Seriosity are analysing these games to see if there are potential applications to the world of work.

Moblogging   Posting blog updates from a mobile device such as a PDA or a cell phone. Allows very quick updates.

Netiquette   Rules/conventions for appropriate behaviour online, e.g. showing respect for other people's privacy.

Netizen   Frequent user of the Internet who also takes responsibility for its use and growth. Cybercitizen is a synonym.

Open Source

A development process, usually associated with software development, in which a computer source code is entered into the public domain and is built upon by distributed users. Modifications are shared with the community. See Open Source Initiative at www.opensource.org, the Mozilla Foundation at www.mozilla. com, and the Linux Foundation at www.linux-foundation.org.

Persistent World

A virtual world environment used as a setting for a role-playing game. Things happen in the world whether a specific player is present or not, e.g. is asleep (like the real world).

Pervasive Computing

The embedding of information and communication devices into the fabric of everyday life (also known as ubiquitous computing).

Plug-in

Usually used in reference to a piece of software that attaches to a main software application and enhances its capabilities. Web browsers often utilize plug-ins to support the use of different types of content, e.g. audio and video.

Podcast

Audio blog. See Blog.

Rich Media

A dynamic media that provides a complex interactive experience through the use of multiple information forms, e.g. text, audio, graphics, video, animation. See Macromedia's Flash, Director, and Shockwave.

RSS

Stands for Really Simple Syndication. Is a format enabling the user to keep up-to-date with changing content in, for example, news sites and blogs. RSS content is read using a feed reader, also known as an aggregator. See Aggregator.

Social Bookmarking

Services letting users store favourite websites online. Users can also share them with others. This supports the process of discovery of new sites and like-minded people. See del.icio.us.

Social Networking

Sites like MySpace, Facebook, and LinkedIn that allow users to build personal profiles that help them connect with others sharing similar interests, skills, or locations. Companies are creating their own internal social networking sites to promote, for example, relationship development with customers, better customer support, locating experts, and forming teams.

Synchronous

Communication happening in real-time, e.g. talking face-to-face or on the telephone.

Tags

Keywords used to describe website content. There are tag-enabled web services for various media, e.g. blog tracking (Technorati), photo sharing (Flickr), social bookmarking (del.icio. us).

Threaded Discussion	An online conference. Users can make multiple responses to a topic. Responses are listed in chronological order.
Virtual Community	A group of people who connect with one another via information and communication technologies to pursue a common interest.
Virtual Community of Practice	A group of people who connect online to pursue a common purpose, usually solving problems in relation to a shared professional activity.
Virtual Organization	Organizational pattern in which distributed individuals, groups, and resources are linked together via computing and communication technologies and groupware.
Virtual World	A computer-based, immersive, and navigable simulated environment. Early virtual worlds were text-based, but now 3D graphics are the norm with interaction between users via avatars. Examples are Second Life, There, Sims Online. In May 2007, the virtual world Entropia was selected by Beijing Municipal People's Government and Cyber Recreation Development.
Vlog	Video blog. See Blog.
VoIP	Voice over Internet Protocol for using the Internet to make telephone calls.

Webcam   A digital camera capable of
                    transmitting real-time images over the
                    Internet.

Weblog   See Blog.

Wi-Fi   Short for 'wireless fidelity'.
                    Technology enabling the transmission
                    of data over wireless networks.

Wiki   A web page that can be edited
                    collaboratively. Take a look at www.
                    wetpaint.com and create your own.